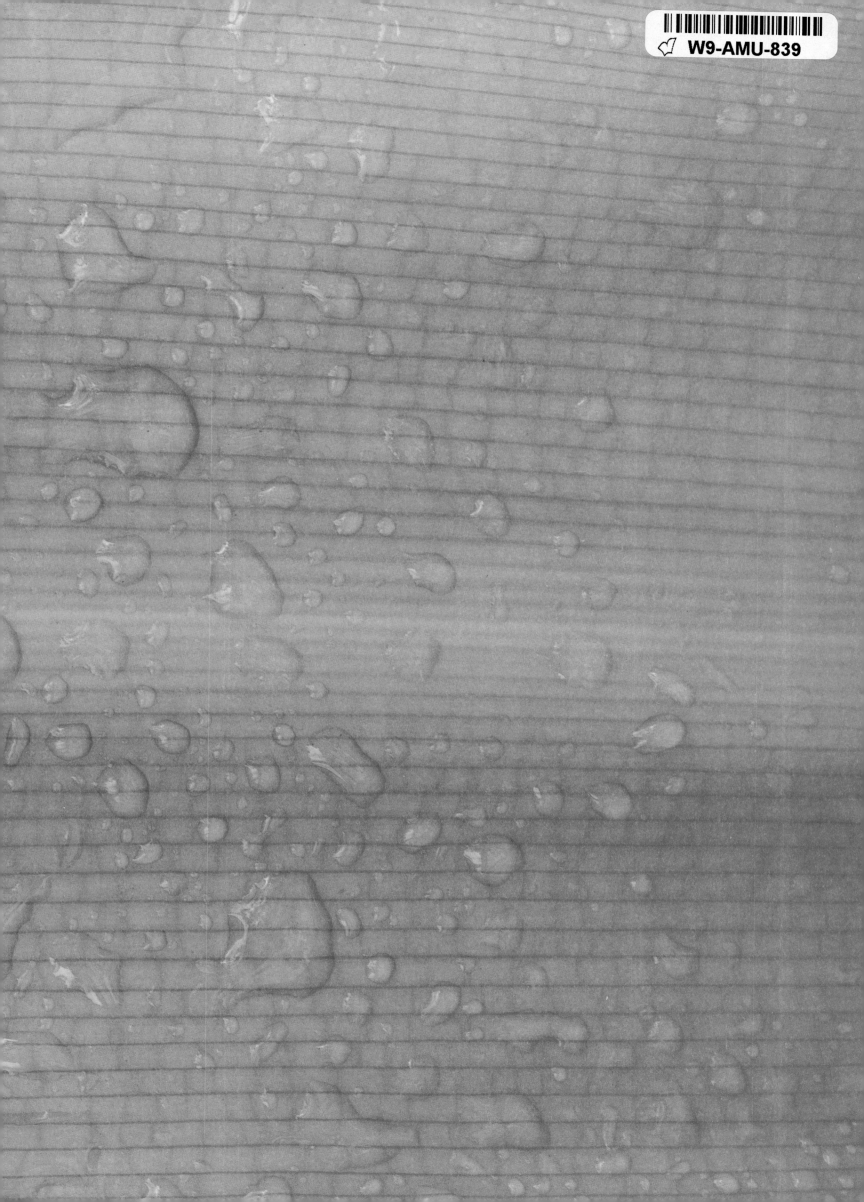

AUSTRALIA'S WILDERNESS HERITAGE

VOLUME 2

FLORA AND FAUNA

AUSTRALIA'S WILDERNESS HERITAGE

VOLUME 2
FLORA AND FAUNA

CONSULTANT EDITORS
TIM FLANNERY   TONY RODD

TEXT
ROBERT COUPE

PHOTOGRAPHY
LEO MEIER

Published in association with the Australian Conservation Foundation

WELDoN
PUBLISHING

SYDNEY • HONG KONG • CHICAGO • LONDON

SPONSORS

The publishers thank the following organisations
for their support in the publication of this book:

Bond Corporation Holdings Limited

Geo Magazine

James Hardie Industries Limited

Qantas Airways Ltd

A Kevin Weldon Production
Published by Weldon Publishing
a division of Kevin Weldon & Associates Pty Limited
372 Eastern Valley Way, Willoughby, NSW 2068, Australia
First published 1988
Reprinted 1989

© Copyright Kevin Weldon & Associates 1988

The illustrations on the slipcase and cases of this publication were
especially commissioned from noted artist Rosemary Ganf.

Consultants: Penelope Figgis, Geoff Mosley
Managing editor: Sheena Coupe
Design and art direction: John Bull, The Book Design Company
Layout and assembly: Stan Lamond, Lesley Workman
Maps: Mike Gorman, Stan Lamond
Production manager: Dianne Leddy
Production consultant: Mick Bagnato

Typeset in Australia by Savage Type, Brisbane
Printed in Australia by The Griffin Press, Adelaide

National Library of Australia Cataloguing-in-Publication Data
Australia's wilderness heritage. Volume 2, Flora and fauna
of world heritage areas.

Bibliography.
Includes index.
ISBN 0 947116 54 0.
ISBN 0 947116 55 9 (set).

1. Wilderness areas – Australia – Pictorial works. 2. Zoology –
Australia – Pictorial works. 3. Botany – Australia – Pictorial works.
4. Australia – Description and travel – 1976 – Views, I. Meier,
Leo, 1951–   . II. Flannery, Timothy Fridtjof. III. Rodd, A.N.
(Anthony Norman). IV. Title: Flora and fauna of world heritage areas.

333.78'2'0994

Pages 2–3

Tranquil subtropical rainforest on the Border Ranges.

Pages 4–5

Pelicans massed in flight over the Gulf Country, Queensland.

Page 6

Cycads and eucalypts, Kings Canyon, Macdonnell Ranges.

Page 7

The koala (*Phascolarctos cinereus*), a unique arboreal marsupial.

Pages 8–9

Mist rises over the rainforest, Downey Creek, Queensland.

Right

Palms, ferns and epiphytes contribute to the rainforest magic,
Lockerbie Scrub, Cape York.

CONTENTS

*S*ugar glider (*Petaurus breviceps*).

15
INTRODUCTION

The Flora and Fauna of:

25
KAKADU AND ARNHEM LAND

53
THE GREAT BARRIER REEF

75
WILLANDRA LAKES

97
WESTERN AND CENTRAL TASMANIA

119
LORD HOWE ISLAND

139
NEW SOUTH WALES RAINFORESTS

163
THE WESTERN ARID REGION

187
THE WET TROPICS

211
THE GREAT SANDY REGION

229
CAPE YORK PENINSULA

253
THE KIMBERLEY

275
SHARK BAY

293
THE EASTERN ARID REGION

311
SOUTHWEST WESTERN AUSTRALIA

333
THE ALPS

353
THE SUBANTARCTIC ISLANDS

375
ANTARCTICA

394
SPONSORS

396
BIBLIOGRAPHY

396
ACKNOWLEDGMENTS

398
INDEX

The flowering centre of a pandani (*Richea pandanifolia*).

Introduction

*W*estern pygmy possum (*Cercartetus concinnus*) feeding on banksia blossom.

THE FLORA OF AUSTRALIA

For the traveller through Australian landscapes, the flora over large areas of the continent is in some ways monotonous. You can travel for hundreds of kilometres seeing only minor or repetitive changes. There are nonetheless gradual changes in composition of the flora as major climatic and soil gradients are traversed. And the monotony is to some extent illusory, in that many additional tree and shrub species are lurking in most areas, but so sparsely that the traveller needs a sharp eye to pick them out. There is often also a rich array of inconspicuous subshrubs, grasses and low herbs.

But there are limited areas of Australia where the flora appears to have run riot. Entering them, you suddenly begin to see one unfamiliar tree or shrub after another, and in the heart of such an area you may be overwhelmed by the diversity of beautiful plants. Some of the world heritage areas described in this book are significant in large part for their flora, although others were chosen for qualities unrelated to flora, such as human prehistory and landforms in Willandra, and marine animals in the Great Barrier Reef. Those heritage areas having a unique and diverse flora as perhaps their most significant element include the wet tropics, the New South Wales rainforests, western Tasmania, Lord Howe Island, southwest Western Australia and the Alps.

What do these areas have in common, that each should harbour such a wealth of plants? This question, it should be obvious, is the same as the question of whether similar historical causes have played a part in the origins of their floras. The answers are not simple.

The exciting development in botanical thinking which has been emerging in recent years is the belief that the major focus of early flowering plant evolution was right here in Australia. The evidence comes not so much from fossils, but from the hierarchies of relationships and distributions which have been painstakingly worked out for some groups of flowering plants as they exist today, combined with the now firmly established timetable of long-term changes in the earth's climate and the break-up of the supercontinent Gondwana.

On the west, South America, Africa, Madagascar and India broke away from Australia as a bloc around 120 million years ago, and shortly afterwards began to split into their present forms. However, South America maintained a connection between its southern tip and Australia via Antarctica, then ice-free, until after the mid-Tertiary (about 30 million years ago).

In a pioneering study of the Proteaceae, one of the most significant flowering plant families of the southern hemisphere, Johnson and Briggs showed convincingly how the major Proteoid subfamily must have arisen in Gondwana before the separation of Africa and Australia. One fragment of its ancestral stock subsequently evolved into the southern African proteas and their relatives. But the greatest diversity of primitive forms exists in eastern Australia. It is now widely accepted that the simplest hypothesis to explain this pattern is that most of the early evolution of the Proteaceae took place here, in the part of Gondwana now called eastern Australia.

It is in Australia's wet tropics that the highest concentration of primitive Proteaceae are to be found, and recent commentators have suggested that these and many other rainforest plants may have survived in approximately this same region with relatively minor evolutionary changes since the time when Gondwana was a single landmass. This assemblage of plants includes, as well as angiosperms, a sprinkling of conifers and cycads, more ancient plant groups believed to have dominated most Gondwana rainforests until about the mid-Tertiary.

The Tasmanian and New South Wales rainforests also harbour many unique forms. Tasmania in particular has a remarkable collection of conifers, for example the Huon pine. Judging by their relationships with conifers of South America and New Zealand, these have survived with only minor changes since the mid-Tertiary but their origins must go back a great deal further. They are acccompanied by angiosperms which also show close links with those of New Zealand and South America, the most notable being the two species of *Nothofagus*. Tasmania also has a more recent alpine flora intruding into its more ancient rainforests.

The temperate and subtropical rainforests of New South Wales are in some respects an impoverished continuation of the wet tropical rainforest, but they also include ancient endemic elements. One such is pinkwood (*Eucryphia moorei*), a decorative small tree of southeastern New South Wales. Only four other species of *Eucryphia* are known, two in Tasmania and two in south Chile. The family Cunoniaceae consists of somewhat primitive trees and shrubs, including the cool temperate *Vesselowskya*, a New South Wales endemic which grows mainly in the beech forests. There are several other examples of apparently primitive, isolated plants in New South Wales rainforests.

Lord Howe Island is a peculiar case. For such a small island its rainforest flora is surprisingly rich. Most of its plants show affinities with those of New Zealand, New Caledonia or north Queensland, rather than those of New South Wales, the closest land. Most major Australian plant groups are entirely absent from its flora but it does have a sprinkling of primitive rainforest forms. The remarkable point about Lord Howe is that it did not exist at all until about 7 million years ago, having risen as a volcano from the ocean floor. A 'stepping-stone' theory must be invoked to account for its flora. Most of the island is so high and rugged that the flora has been little affected by human impact, but there is a growing danger in the form of invasive introduced trees and shrubs.

Southwest Western Australia is the outstanding region in Australia for diversity of sclerophyll vegetation. This consists essentially of light-loving plants with small leaves that contain a high proportion of lignified tissues. There has been debate about why sclerophyll flora has proliferated in most parts of Australia. The traditional explanation was that these are drought-resistant forms which evolved as a response to an increasingly arid climate in the Miocene epoch, perhaps around 15 million years ago. A more recent view is that sclerophyll appeared initially in quite wet areas as a response to the increasing impoverishment of soils due to long-term leaching out of nutrients.

In the southwest of Western Australia an explosive burst of evolution seems to have taken place, most of it after the southwest flora became isolated from that of the east by increasing aridity. A large number of plant genera have both eastern and southwestern species, though usually none common to both; a repeating pattern is for the southwestern species to greatly outnumber the eastern, and to include more bizarre and colourful forms.

The thick tangle of foliage and undergrowth in a tropical rainforest, Lockerbie Scrub, Cape York.

Just why the southwestern flora should be so much richer is something of a puzzle. One explanation is that fluctuations in climate have placed pressure on the plants to come up with adaptations to adversity, but have also opened up new and expanding environments such as sand-drifts, saline depressions and boggy ground. Bursts of evolution followed by contraction or displacement have over time resulted in a rich pattern, with many plants clinging to a precarious existence in refuge areas.

The Australian Alps is the stronghold of another unique flora. The most interesting point about our alpine vegetation is that, in the context of Australian vegetation history, it is extremely recent and appears still to be evolving. It seems likely that the present flora has largely replaced an earlier mountain flora of purely Gondwana origin dominated by *Nothofagus* and conifers (of which the mountain plum-pine, *Podocarpus lawrencei*, is a remnant). Fossil evidence shows that *Nothofagus* may have been present in the Mt Kosciusko area as few as 35 000 years ago. This temperate rainforest flora is thought to have disappeared from the Alps due to a combination of mountain uplift which began towards the end of the Tertiary (about 2.5 million years ago), and the cooling and drying of the climate which took place especially during the Pleistocene glaciations, the last of which ended only about 10 000 years ago.

Most of the colourful alpine flora consists of immigrant elements from other cool areas of the world, some apparently arriving in Australia in very recent times. Migratory birds were probably the principal agents of introduction. But there is also an important element derived from older Australian sclerophyll groups, which appear to have colonised the Alps from below, evolving new forms as they moved upward. Examples of these are the alpine epacrids, grevilleas and bush-peas, not to mention the snow gums.

The picture of the origins of the Australian flora sketched here is one of long isolation, first in Gondwana, later in Australia alone. Some recent migrant elements are widespread, but are overshadowed by the ancient endemic elements, which are most richly developed and preserved in some of the world heritage areas described. The long isolation has resulted in many very stable ecosystems, with delicate balances maintained between species. The most disastrous impacts on these ecosystems since white settlement have been from introduced plants and animals, clearing of forests and addition of nutrients to soils. Mining, logging and urban development have had lesser impacts, though these have been highly significant in some more critical areas.

TONY RODD

*S*weet pittosporum (*Pittosporum undulatum*).
Right *F*lowering shrubs, D'Entrecasteaux National Park, Western Australia.

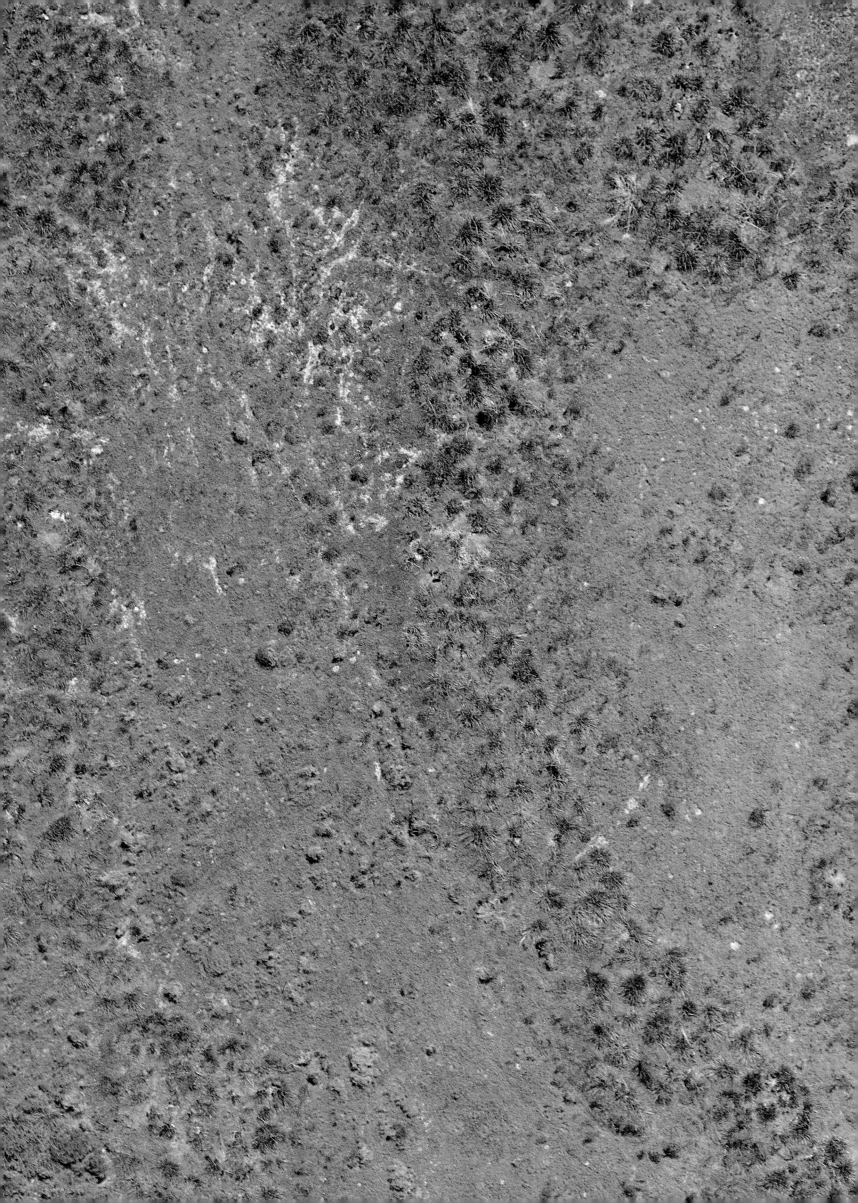

THE FAUNA OF AUSTRALIA

For millions of years Australia has been isolated on the far side of the earth from the other great landmasses. On our continent, evolution has taken a separate path, what amounts to a second experiment in the evolutionary process. Because of Australia's unique origins and long isolation, the experiment has resulted in a different and very distinctive fauna. Kangaroos and emus fill Australia's plains, in stark contrast to the hoofed animals and their predators that are found almost everywhere else. Our trees are filled with parrots and honeyeaters rather than the woodpeckers and orioles of other lands.

From its earliest discovery the fauna of Australia has thrilled and fascinated visitors from other continents. Many of the new species, although strange, seemed vaguely familiar. Thus our language abounds with marsupial 'moles', native 'cats' and Tasmanian 'tigers'. Other species were, however, totally strange to European eyes and to this day are the subject of scientific research. Only in the last few years have we realised that the strangest of animals, the platypus, finds its food with an electrosensitive bill, or that the night parrot, an owl-like species which was thought extinct for many years, still survives in a remote part of central Australia. From Charles Darwin's time to the present, such studies of Australian animals continue to reveal the complex and intricate workings of evolution.

But the delights of observing and studying fauna are not reserved merely for the scientist. Exploration of the natural environment is becoming an increasingly important part of the leisure activities of many Australians. After 200 years more and more European Australians are beginning to awaken to the treasure trove of their natural heritage and to explore for themselves the environment that nurtures us all. Australians are privileged in the diversity of environments that are available for them to explore within their continent, which includes almost all the environments available on Planet Earth. This diversity is the result of changes in Australia's climate over millions of years.

Some 50 million years ago, when Australia and Antarctica were a single landmass, Australia was covered with vast, uniform temperate forests. Their remnants survive today in southwest Tasmania and southeastern Australia. Most are Antarctic beech forests, tiny fragments preserved in the most favourable or sheltered spots. Because of the long isolation and fragmentation of these forests, almost all the larger animals that once inhabited them are now extinct. However, some of the smaller animals, such as the Tasmanian cave spider, remain as reminders of the diverse fauna that must once have inhabited the forests.

By 15 million years ago Australia had broken away from Antarctica and drifted into warmer latitudes. Tropical and subtropical rainforest began to replace the temperate forest and a range of animal species exploited the new habitats. Today, substantial tracts of these forests remain in the Atherton–Daintree area of north Queensland. Species such as the green ringtail, musky rat-kangaroo and Lumholtz's tree-kangaroo survive in these forests today. That they were once far more widespread is verified by the fossils of related species, many millions of years old, that have been found in places as distant from north Queensland as western Victoria,

Boyd's forest dragon (*Gonocephalus boydii*),
an endemic species of the wet tropics.

central Australia and the Gulf of Carpentaria. Although the rainforests are among the most diverse of Australian habitats, they are a mere shadow of their former selves and their fauna can rightly be regarded as 'living fossils'.

Today, Australia's rainforest relicts are surrounded by belts of more open vegetation, often wet sclerophyll forest. These forests appeared sometime after 15 million years ago as Australia, after first warming, began to dry out. The crowns of the trees in sclerophyll forests do not form a continuous canopy; more light reaches the forest floor so that grasses and other plants can grow there. Herbivores such as kangaroos no longer needed to climb trees to find enough food, so tree-kangaroos were replaced by the ground-dwelling kangaroos and wallabies familiar to modern Australians. The possums faced severe problems, as they could not simply climb from one treetop to the next. Many rainforest species were replaced by gliding species. Gliding has evolved independently many times during possum evolution, which indicates the usefulness of the adaptation.

As time went on, however, even these tall forests could not survive the drying out of the continent and were replaced by woodland, savannah and desert. Only the most versatile of possums could survive in such environments, and only one, the brushtail possum, is at all common in these habitats. Found in almost every suburban backyard in Australia, and inhabiting tree hollows from Alice Springs to Cairns, the brushtail is perhaps the most versatile and well known of all marsupials.

Although the drying out spelled doom for many animals that were dependent on forest habitats, it allowed other groups to expand dramatically. Among the birds, the emu, malleefowl and the tiny desert wrens all rapidly exploited the new, dry environments. Mammals such as kangaroos, marsupial mice and some small, unusual species such as the marsupial mole also found homes. Indeed, today, many of what are thought of as typically Australian animals, for example the red kangaroo and emu, are typical of the dry centre.

Unhappily, it is also the arid environments that have suffered most since the coming of Europeans. Remarkably, as far as we know, not a single rainforest animal species has become extinct in Australia over the past 200 years. However, sixteen mammals and one bird have disappeared forever from the drier environments, many from the desert. Just why the deserts were so vulnerable is difficult to tell. A delicate balance had been struck between Aborigines and their environment. Their burning patterns ensured that wildfires would not blacken vast areas of country and that a patchwork of old vegetation (providing shelter) and newly burned areas (providing food) existed side by side. With the removal of the Aborigines, and the introduction of sheep, cattle, rabbit and fox, many species simply vanished.

However, this does not account for all the losses. The thylacine in Tasmania and toolache wallaby in South Australia seem to have been hunted into oblivion, while other species were collected once or twice in the early years of settlement, then never heard of again. They remind us just how fragile our natural heritage is, and how incompletely we understand it. We must ensure that in our continuing tenure of Australia we do not add to the list of species that are lost forever. The listing of the heritage areas that are the subject of this book is one of the most important tools available to us in achieving this.

TIM FLANNERY

The comb-crested jacana or lotus bird (*Irediparra gallinacea*) is a long-legged wading bird.

Kakadu and
Arnhem Land

Kakadu and Arnhem Land

*S*crew pines (*Pandanus spiralis*) silhouetted against a Kakadu skyline.

Previous pages
A saltwater crocodile (*Crocodylus porosus*) displays its ferocious jaws.

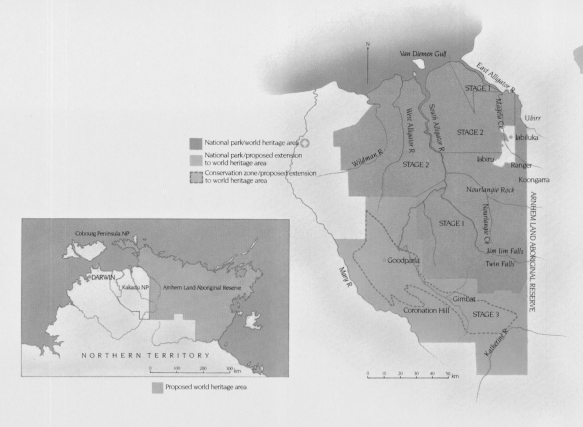

National park/world heritage area
National park/proposed extension to world heritage area
Conservation zone/proposed extension to world heritage area

Proposed world heritage area

ecause of Kakadu's recently acquired popularity as a tourist destination, much media coverage of the area has focused on the prevalence of the large and dangerous saltwater crocodile. This narrow emphasis has tended to obscure the fact that the region can boast an abundance and diversity of wildlife that is among the richest in Australia.

The saltwater crocodile is only one of about a hundred known species of reptiles and amphibians found in Kakadu. Among the others are many species of snakes, including three extremely venomous species, which, however, are rarely encountered by human visitors. As well, there are many different lizards, some of them brightly coloured, more than twenty species of frogs and five species of freshwater turtles.

The diversity of habitats within Kakadu has contributed to a great concentration of birdlife in the area. The most abundant are the waterbirds, which thrive in the swamps and lagoons. Kakadu National Park probably contains the world's richest breeding grounds for tropical waterbirds.

The region's mammals, comprising more than fifty species, include a large number of marsupials, ranging from the largest, the antilopine wallaroo, to the tiny Harney's marsupial mouse, a recently discovered species that is restricted to Arnhem Land. Just over half of Kakadu's mammal species are bats, including several endangered species.

Because of its great diversity of physical environments — taking in open woodland, eucalypt forest, isolated patches of rainforests, floodplains, swamps, dry grassland plains and rocky hills — Kakadu supports an enormous range of plantlife and vegetation types. Many of the area's flowering plants are still poorly known; others are still being discovered. Some of these plants, especially the aquatic ones, have been damaged by the water buffalo, which was introduced in the nineteenth century. Several noxious weeds, especially the fern *Salvinia molesta* and the South American *Mimosa pigra*, are now established in the park and pose a serious threat to much of the plantlife and associated fauna.

The seeds of the red lotus lily (*Nelumbo nucifera*) are eaten by Aborigines. It thrives in the permanent swamps of Kakadu's wetlands but has suffered from the introduction of buffaloes. In recent times its numbers have increased.

Below

Although Kakadu's wetlands provide an ideal habitat for pied stilts (*Himantopus himantopus*), these long-legged small birds are well distributed around the continent. They are usually seen in small flocks and build nests in mud hollows.

When it takes to the water the darter (*Anhinga melanogaster*) swims strongly with only its head and long snaky neck visible. On emerging it spreads its powerful wings to allow its water-soaked plumage to dry. The darter is spectacular in flight, soaring high in the air and moving in spirals. It feeds mainly on fish, which it stalks and spears with its sharp bill, and nests in trees whose branches overhang water. The bird shown here is a female; the male is almost completely black.

*A*mong the most primitive of waterfowl and now confined to Australia's extreme north, the magpie goose (*Anseranas semipalmata*) was once found as far south as Melbourne. Although it is still abundant, its numbers declined as buffaloes grazed on the vegetation that is an important source of food. The magpie goose's habitat is now threatened by the spread of the mimosa weed.

*I*n the dry season the magpie goose uses its hook-tipped bill to unearth spike-rush bulbs. In the wet season it will often dive to gather food from the bottom of the swamp.

*T*he knob on the head of the magpie goose grows larger as the bird ages and is often less pronounced in the female goose.

30

*G*rowing to just over half a metre in length, the glossy ibis (*Plegadis falcinellus*) is the smallest of all Australian ibises. It gets its name from the shimmering blue-green of its wings, which from a distance blends with the predominantly reddish brown colouration of its body. The glossy ibis uses it long slender bill to delve beneath the water or into mud.

Left

*U*ntil it was protected by law the great egret (*Egretta alba*) was widely hunted for the long white plumes that in the breeding season grow on its back, extending below the tail. When it flies, the great egret's long legs extend straight behind it. When not airborne, these legs carry this handsome bird into mud or shallow water where it forages for fish, frogs and insects.

Despite its fearsome reputation the taipan (*Oxyuranus scutellatus*), one of the world's largest venomous snakes, is more likely to retire than to attack if faced with an aggressor. But when cornered it lashes out with agile and deadly ferocity. It is mainly active during the day and feeds almost entirely on warm-blooded animals.

This Gilbert's dragon (*Lophognathus gilberti*) displays the large patch of white on the lower jaw which is peculiar to males of the species in the far north. This lizard grows to about half a metre long and is often found perched on tree limbs. The female lays its eggs under leaf litter and leaves them to hatch.

A rather discomfiting head-on view of a saltwater crocodile (*Crocodylus porosus*), the larger and more intimidating of the two species of Australian crocodiles. This species grows normally to just under five metres long and is found in coastal waters, river estuaries and, less commonly, upstream in freshwater rivers. It preys on vertebrate animals.

*T*he saltwater crocodile has powerful jaws which contain strong, sharp teeth. When air-breathing prey is seized it is held under the water until it drowns, and is then swallowed whole or broken up into large pieces.

*R*ows of jagged subcutaneous back plates, called osteoderms, are a characteristic of all crocodiles.

The sand goanna (*Varanus panoptes*) is one of more than half a dozen species of goanna found in Kakadu and is one of the region's largest lizards. It is similar in size and colour to the much more widespread Gould's goanna, but is restricted largely to the sedgelands.

Above

The northern white-lipped dragon (*Lophognathus temporalis*) is so named because of the broad white stripe that extends along its jaw and body. It is also known as the northern water dragon because of its preference for moist habitats.

In a striking display of defiance, the frilled lizard (*Chlamydosaurus kingii*) opens its mouth, causing its frill, which usually lies flat against its neck, to flare out menacingly. This dragon is very common throughout most of northern Australia.

Above

Known to scientists only since 1977, but long familiar to Aborigines, the Oenpelli python (*Morelia oenpelliensis*) is endemic to the stony regions of the Kakadu escarpment. A nocturnal hunter of mammals and birds, it spends its days in rocks and crevices, where its colours provide effective camouflage, or in tree branches.

The olive python (*Liasis olivaceus*) is distinguished by its uniform olive brown colour and shimmering scales. This large nocturnal snake is confined to the north of the continent where it inhabits woodland regions or stony habitats, especially in the vicinity of rocky hills and ranges.

Curcuma australasica blooms in the gorges of the escarpment.

Right
Dew drops are attracted to the leaf hairs of this small prostrate plant, *Trianthema megasperma*. Endemic to the Kakadu–Oenpelli region, it was recognised as a distinct species and named in 1983.

Below
The bloom of this violet (*Hybanthus enneaspermus*) has one petal much larger than the others.

Right
The flowering head of the purple clover weed (*Uraria cylindracea*) lengthens as the wet season progresses. This annual herb, which grows to about fifty centimetres high, is a late bloomer throughout the woodland regions of Kakadu.

Far right
The masses of red flowers, with their uncurling styles, make for easy recognition of Dryander's grevillea (*Grevillea dryandri*), which grows as a shrub reaching almost a metre high. It is found widely throughout northern Australia and in Kakadu is a plant of the sandstone plateau.

The velvet-leaved fig (*Ficus leucotricha*) is widely scattered across the far north of Australia. Sandstone ledges and ravines are its characteristic habitats.

Above

*I*n monsoon forests the banyan (*Ficus virens*) sends down numerous aerial roots from its branches. Some thicken to form additional trunks.

Left

A rotting fallen log and leaf litter on the floor of a monsoon forest. The yellow-brown patches are bracket fungi, the shiny green leaves that are beginning to grow over the log belong to a yam (*Discorea* sp.), and the other trailing plants are one of the jasmines (*Jasminum* sp.).

The striking yellow of flowering wattle bushes (*Acacia* sp.) stands out against the greyish browns of the boulders and the predominant green of the vegetation that grows in the vicinity of the escarpment and on the sandstone plateau. Hardy and opportunistic plants, wattles are able to take root in rocky environments, turning to advantage the sand and decomposed leaf litter that constitute the only available soil in many crevices and depressions.

The many species of wattles that grow on Kakadu's sandstone escarpment fall into two main groups: those which, like the plant here, bear long fluffy spikes; and those whose flowers are like yellow balls of cottonwool.

*D*espite having shorter necks, legs and bills than most herons, nankeeen night herons (*Nycticorax caledonicus*) are efficient nocturnal predators on fish and other aquatic creatures all around Australia. In the north these birds breed during the wet season. They are particularly numerous in the monsoonal forests where they roost during the day on tree branches, never far from water.

*F*reshwater lagoons with a plentiful supply of waterlilies are the favourite haunt of the green pygmy goose (*Nettapus pulchellus*). This duck, confined mainly to the extreme north of the continent and New Guinea, feeds on aquatic plants. It is a strong flier and swimmer, but is rarely seen on land, preferring to perch on the exposed parts of sunken logs.

Below
*T*he swamphen (*Porphryio porphryio*) has long, spreading toes which enable it to walk on waterlilies. A bright red shield protects the bird's face as it forages for reed shoots, which it breaks off with its bill and then holds, like a cockatoo, in its foot.

*T*he patterned black, spoon-shaped bill of the royal spoonbill (*Platalea regia*) enables this large bird to scoop up fish and other small aquatic creatures as it wades through swamps and lagoons. Except for a small red patch on the forehead, its plumage is white, in sharp contrast to the black of its legs, face and bill.

*R*arely seen, drab-coloured, guttural-voiced, awkward in flight and solitary in its habits, the great-billed heron (*Ardea sumatrana*) lives and breeds in the mangrove swamps of northern Australia and tropical Asia. It grows to just over a metre long and feeds on aquatic animals.

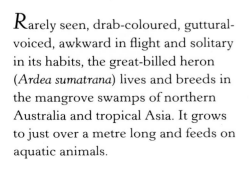

In Australia the little kingfisher (*Ceyx pusillus*) occurs in Cape York and at the extreme north of Arnhem Land. These tiny, brilliant, but very elusive birds live among mangroves and along running streams in rainforests.

This immature pied heron (*Ardea picata*) displays only the early signs of the black head and crest feathers that will distinguish its adult plumage. Northern Australia is the southern extremity of this bird's range. It lives in swamps and grasslands, eats insects and invertebrates, and scavenges for meat around areas of human habitation.

*T*he Burdekin duck (*Tadorna radjah*) is distinguished by the chestnut and black colouration of its back and shoulders, the chestnut band around its breast, and the loud rattle and hoarse whistling sounds that usually herald its approach. It inhabits aquatic environments in far northern Australia and New Guinea.

*T*he plumed whistling duck (*Dendrocygna eytoni*) is distributed widely across northern and eastern Australia but is concentrated in the tropics. It appears more at home on land than in water and feeds mainly in open grassland. It is named for the plumes that grow from its flanks and the constant whistling sound it makes while in flight.

The thick-bodied and flabby-skinned file snake (*Acrochordus arafurae*) lives almost exclusively in the water and is out of its element on land. Its favoured habitats are freshwater pools and rivers where it preys nocturnally on fish, often with its tail wrapped around tree roots. The flesh of this non-venomous snake is eaten by Aborigines.

The northern snake-necked turtle (*Chelodina rugosa*) is named for its long thin neck, which broadens into a wide flat head and is retracted into the shell with a slithering sideways movement. It is one of the most common of several species of turtles encountered in Kakadu, where it lives in still or gently flowing water and preys on fish and crustaceans.

The subtle colour gradations of the tiny saxicoline tree frog (*Litoria coplandi*) blend with its rocky habitats in north and northwest Australia. It spends its days hidden among rocks and comes out at night to visit nearby still water.

A northern dwarf tree frog (*Litoria bicolor*) has its vocal sac distended as it emits its high-pitched mating call. This small frog, which does not exceed three centimetres in length, is an exceptionally agile jumper. It inhabits streams and swamps across most of northern Australia.

Below
*T*he large-eyed and ornate burrowing frog (*Limnodynastes ornatus*) is often found in drier sandy regions.

Below
*G*reen tree frogs (*Litoria caerulea*) mating. The female possesses the bright green colour of this very familiar species, which occurs in widely differing habitats throughout the north. The male exhibits the olive brown hues that these frogs sometimes assume.

Right

A hairy and spiny-legged garden orb-weaver (*Eriophora transmarinus*) spins its intricately structured web.

Below

Among the myriad insects found in the Kakadu National Park are colourful shield bugs (family Scutelleridae) (*top left*), plant-suckers that live off a range of vegetation types; long-horned grasshoppers (family Tettigoniidae), such as the bright green katydid (*Caedicia* sp.) (*top right*); and short-horned grasshoppers, two of which are shown in copulation (*bottom left*). The beetle (*bottom right*) is a scarab beetle of the subfamily Melanthinae, small black or brown beetles that live off plant roots.

Right

Short-horned grasshoppers such as the one shown here, *Petasida ephiphigera*, are often brilliantly coloured and even in the same species colours may differ widely.

Below

These three photographs show a fully grown cicada nymph (*Macrotristria* sp.) shedding its brown outer skin on the stem of a forest plant to emerge as a winged adult. Newly hatched cicadas burrow beneath the soil where they can live for several years on the sap of tree roots. When a nymph comes out of the soil, it climbs on to a tree or other vertical object where it casts off the brittle skin by splitting it along the back.

*A*lthough smaller than the red kangaroo, the antilopine wallaroo (*Macropus antilopinus*) closely resembles it. This wallaroo is easily the largest macropod found in the Kakadu National Park. It is confined to the extreme north of the continent and is unusual among wallaroos in that it is often seen in large groups.

Below

*P*erhaps the most conspicuous of the feral animals in Kakadu is the water buffalo (*Bubalus bubalis*) which was introduced from Indonesia in the early nineteenth century as a draught animal and for its meat.

*T*he dingo (*Canis familiaris dingo*) is also an introduced animal but, because of its thousands of years of residence, is not considered feral. Nevertheless it does take its toll on native birds and mammals, on which it preys voraciously. Unlike many other areas, dingoes in Kakadu have little interaction with domestic dogs and crossbreeding is extremely rare.

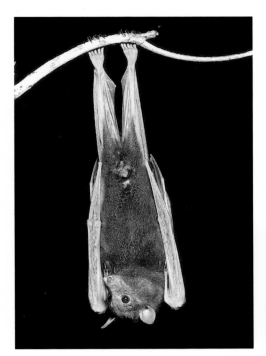

The little red flying fox (*Pteropus scapulatus*) is one of two species of flying foxes that are commonly encountered in Kakadu, noisily feeding on fruits and flowers.

Below
The northern quoll (*Dasyurus hallucatus*) favours rocky habitats.

The brush-tailed phascogale (*Phascogale tapoatafa*), seen here devouring a large insect, is, like the northern quoll, one of the dasyurids — a family of small, carnivorous marsupial mammals. Whereas the northern quoll is confined to the north of Australia and largely avoids trees, the brush-tailed phascogale is arboreal and is distributed widely, but in limited areas, around the coast.

*T*he blue-winged kookaburra (*Dacelo leachii*) inhabits forested areas in the far north, and the northeast and northwest coastal areas.

*A*ustralia's only stork, the black-necked stork, or jabiru, (*Xenorhynchus asiaticus*) is, unlike most other storks, solitary in its habits. Although also found along the east coast, it is much more common in the north.

*B*rolgas (*Grus rubicundus*) are noted for their elaborate dance-like rituals which are celebrated in Aboriginal folklore and imitated in some corroborees. These large grey cranes grow to more than a metre high. They inhabit swampy areas in northern and eastern Australia and are seen in large numbers in many parts of Kakadu. Brolgas are also known for their longevity; individuals are known to have lived for up to sixty years.

The Great
Barrier Reef

The Great
Barrier Reef

Sacoglossan sea slug (*Cyerce nigricans*) feeding on turtle weed, *Chlorodesmis*.

Previous pages
Divers silhouetted against an overhanging reef.

The wealth and variety of its marine fauna is the great glory of the Great Barrier Reef. The series of reefs that stretch for almost 2000 kilometres along the coast of north Queensland play host to a bewildering array of marine lifeforms and together constitute one of the world's richest and most diverse marine ecosystems.

Corals, which are living animals, are the basic lifeform of the reefs. There are almost 400 different species of coral in the Great Barrier Reef. Some, such as the large brain corals, grow into huge boulder-like masses; others form spreading crusts on the surface of the reef; still others are fragile flower-like shapes whose beauty belies their predatory nature. The diversity of shapes, forms and colours which these corals exhibit is indicated in many of the descriptive popular names that are applied to them. Corals are referred to as fans, whips, baskets, daisies, mushrooms, cups, staghorns, needles and buttons. Many of these are visible from the surface; others, including the fan-shaped and intricately filigreed gorgonian corals grow mainly in deeper waters, out of sight of all but divers.

Sharing this environment are thousands of other species of marine animals, many of them, like the corals, displaying a wild extravagance of shapes and colours. Well over 1500 species of fish inhabit these waters and again their popular names provide a clue to the suggestiveness of their form and colour. There are butterfly fish, clown fish, scorpion fish, potato cods, trumpet fish and a host of others. Crustaceans, molluscs, marine worms, clams and echinoderms contribute further to the colour and variety of the marine fauna.

Many of the more stable coral cays that have formed throughout the reef area have developed some form of vegetation. This ranges from a few low struggling shrubs on smaller islands to substantial stands of pisonia trees and screw pines on some of the larger ones. These islands also support often vast colonies of seabirds which find on them relatively safe nesting sites. Shearwaters, gannets, gulls, frigatebirds and especially terns are among the prominent varieties of seabirds.

The black-barred fish in this nocturnal photograph are cardinal fish (*Apogon aureus*). The pink-coloured fish in the middle of the group is a fairy basslet (*Anthias squampinnis*), while the partly obscured larger, red fish is a squirrel fish (*Myripristis* sp.). Both cardinal and squirrel fish spend their days in the security of underwater caves and venture out at night to feed.

*T*he potato cod (*Epinephelus tukula*) is one of the largest fish on the Great Barrier Reef. Despite its bulk, the pugnacious set of its jaw and the hugeness of its mouth, it is not aggressive to humans. It even takes an occasional benign interest in the exploits of divers. It is, however, rarely encountered nowadays and is protected in Australian waters. This specimen is estimated to weigh almost fifty kilograms.

*W*ith its several rings of bright yellow tentacles extended, the daisy coral, *Tubastrea aurea*, draws a fish which has been paralysed by the coral's stinging cells towards its central mouth. Among the most eye-catching of the hard corals — those that have a solid limestone skeleton — daisy corals display their tentacles during the day as well as at night. However, as they grow mainly in sheltered areas away from bright light, only divers can experience their beauty at first hand.

As the butterfly cod (*Pterois volitans*) wafts slowly through the water it spreads its long trailing pectoral fins in brilliant display. This fish is protected from would-be predators by the extremely venomous spines that protrude from its back and are concealed within the fins. Despite its usual leisurely movements, it is an agile nocturnal and diurnal predator on small fish and crustaceans. The butterfly cod grows to almost forty centimetres long. It inhabits the waters off the north Australian coast and extends throughout the Indo–Pacific region, and is most commonly seen in the vicinity of coral or rocky reefs.

The feathery, wafting and delicately hued tentacles of the spiral tubeworm (family Serpulidae) are used for respiration and for gathering plankton. These tentacles will retract swiftly into the worm's protective tube at the approach of a potential predator. This worm belongs to the group of very beautiful and variously coloured sedentary marine worms that include the fanworms, featherduster worms and Christmas tree worms. These polychaetes secrete tubes that attach to rock or coral. As the coral grows the tubes become embedded in it.

Colonies of Christmas tree worms (*Spirobranchus giganteus*), named for the shapes which protrude from the tubes in which they live, can produce a riot of colour on an area of coral. Individual worms can produce offspring of widely differing colours. Young worms bore into the coral, establish their tubes and then continue to grow at the same rate as the coral to avoid being sealed in.

A black clown anemone fish (*Amphiprion melanopus*), one of eight species of this genus found in Australian waters, among the anemone tentacles which offer it security but whose stinging tentacles spell death to most other fish species. Brightly coloured and distinctively patterned *Amphiprion* species are among the most commonly encountered reef fish.

*A*n anemone fish (*Amphiprion peridaraion*) peers out from the safety of anemone tentacles. Away from this protective environment these brilliant reef dwellers are an easy prey for larger marine carnivores. Anemone fish are hermaphrodites, being born male and changing into females when they mature. Not surprisingly, females are always larger than males.

Cowries are noted and prized for their beautiful shells. The mantles which cover these shells as the animals move over the coral at night to feed on sponges and other small animals are often even more spectacular. This species of small cowry, *Cypraea cribraria*, is remarkable for the brilliance of its orange mantle.

The fleshy mantles which cover the shell openings of clams (*Tridacna* spp.) display a remarkable variety of colours. Most clams are seen on sand or on the top of coral. The one shown here, the boring clam (*Tridacna crocea*), embeds itself firmly in hard coral, leaving only its mantle visible. One of the smaller species of the genus, it grows to a maximum length of about fifteen centimetres.

Perhaps the most conspicuous of the many asteroids on the Great Barrier Reef, the blue sea star (*Linckia laevigata*) inhabits shallow waters and spreads its five radiating arms during the day. Most sea stars are carnivores and feed on corals, worms and molluscs through the mouth on the underside of the central disc. While many sea stars are capable of sprouting new arms if broken in two, the blue sea star can regenerate a new body from one severed arm.

The aptly named painted spiny lobster (*Panulirus versicolor*) is the most brightly coloured of several large crayfish that inhabit the reef. It is much sought after for its meat, but has proved difficult to catch. It spends most of the day hidden in rock or coral crevices and comes out at night to prey on other marine animals, both live and dead.

Despite their plant-like appearance, sponges are animals. They are collections of living cells, which adhere together around skeletons of calcium or silica and attach themselves to underwater surfaces. Seawater is drawn through pores, providing the sponge with the nutrients it needs to survive.

A male and female lesser frigatebird (*Fregata ariel*) in the branches of a pisonia tree. The male's red throat is inflated like a large balloon as part of a courtship ritual. These large birds breed on islands around the coast of northern Australia. They generally build their nests of sticks in the branches of trees. They are superb in flight but reluctant to enter the water, preferring to swoop and pick off small fish, invertebrates and molluscs from the surface.

*T*he leaves (*top*) of the pandanus (*Pandanus heronensis*), growing in spiral clusters around the slender trunk and branches, have given rise to the popular name, screw pine. The tree's large pineapple-like fruit (*above*) is both sweet-smelling and sweet to the taste. Large cream-coloured flowers give way to clusters of green fruit which in turn mature to a bright orange colour. The long, rigid and spiky leaves surrounding the fruit are characteristic of the pandanus.

The spreading bright green shrub *Scaevola taccada*, commonly known as fan flower, is shown here growing through the rubble on Fairfax Island near the southern extremity of the Great Barrier Reef. This is one of several species of shrubs that manage to thrive in the botanically inhospitable conditions existing on many of the coral cays.

A large colony of seabirds nesting on Michaelmas Cay near Cairns in part of the Great Barrier Reef Marine Park. Large numbers of birds on cays can present a threat to some species of plants which are either trampled or taken for nesting material.

Below

Eastern reef egrets (*Egretta sacra*) are wading birds that build their platform nests either on the ground or, as here, in tree branches.

The sticky seeds of the pisonia tree (*Pisonia grandis*) help bind together the leaves and grasses with which the black noddy (*Anous minutus*) builds its nest.

A crested tern (*Sterna bergii*) in its simple nest, scooped out among ground vegetation, cries out in alarm at the approach of a photographer. This most common of Australian terns breeds all around the mainland and Tasmanian coasts, mainly on offshore islands, including coral cays.

The brown booby (*Sula leucogaster*) builds its nest of twigs and leaves predominantly in areas of sparse vegetation, such as the site shown here on Fairfax Island. It is common around the continent's northern shores and often ranges far out to sea in search of food. Two or three pale green eggs are laid and pale grey chicks, which are vulnerable to attack by gulls, are hatched. As they grow the chicks develop white plumage. The adult bird is a male. The female's beak has a greenish tinge.

Mushroom coral

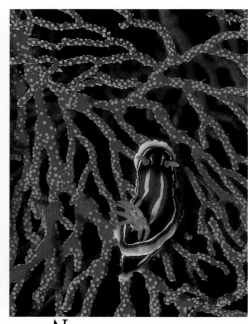

Nudibranch on gorgonian

Some of the many different types of true coral and gorgonian coral that are found on the Great Barrier Reef. Mushroom corals (*Fungia* sp.), are unusual in that they are large solitary polyps which do not remain attached to the reef. Brain corals are hard corals. They are named because they resemble, in overall shape and in the maze-like pattern of rises and depressions, the human brain. Long, irregularly meandering lines of polyps jointly form walls and create the mountain-ridge effect that the close-up, of the species *Leptoria phrygia*, shows. The other four photographs show some of the gorgonian corals, characterised by branching structures that create arresting filigree effects. They form the distinctive group of corals, often highly coloured, that are popularly known as either sea fans or sea whips. The skeletal structure of gorgonian corals, which determines their shape, consists of a core of protein known as gorgonin. Shown in close-up (*bottom right*) are some of the tiny polyps that cluster in vast numbers on this structure.

Sea fan or gorgonian

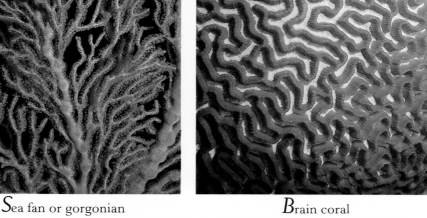

Brain coral

Sea fan or gorgonian

Polyps of a sea fan

Right
This large expanse of hard purple coral (*Montipora tuberculosa*), deep down in a sheltered pool, has grown as a crust over the reef surface, covering other species of coral in its spread. *Montipora tuberculosa* is one of several species of encrusting corals. Some species grow in thin leaf-like plates and are known as foliose species.

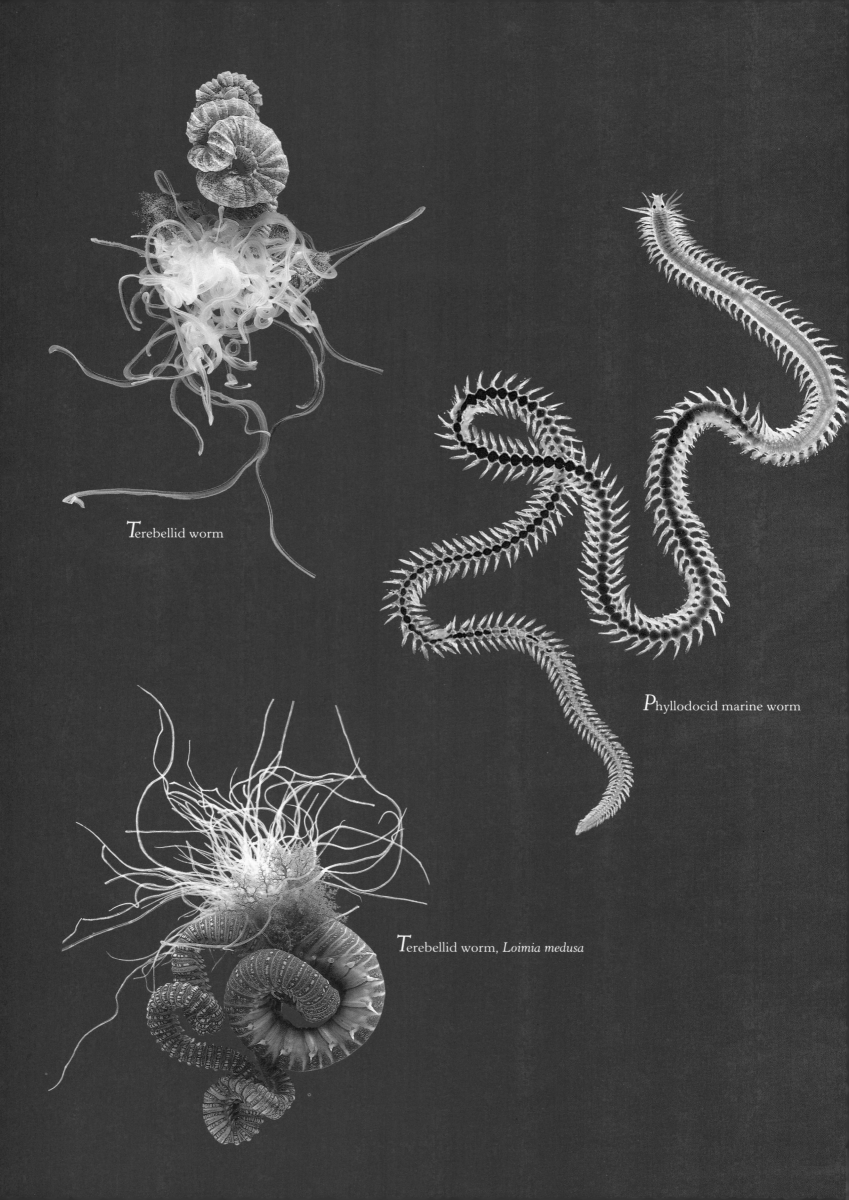

Terebellid worm

Phyllodocid marine worm

Terebellid worm, *Loimia medusa*

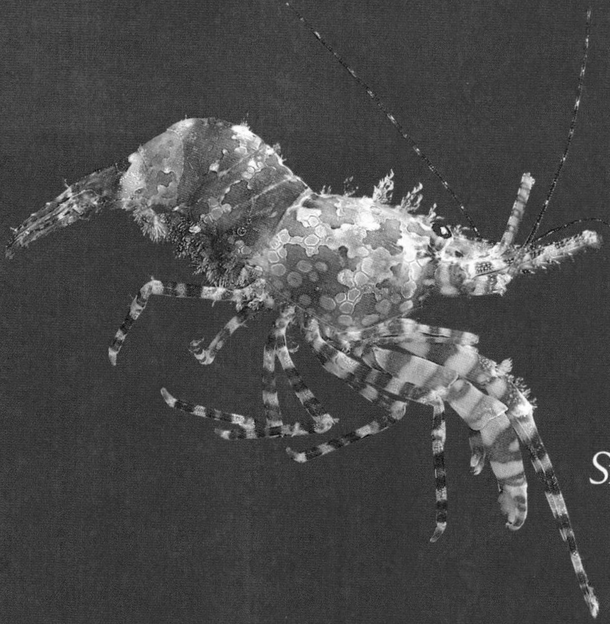

Shrimp

Ram's horn shell (*Spirula spirula*)
colonised by goose barnacles

Mantis shrimp

Previous pages
A selection of marine invertebrates: terebellid worms are tube-dwellers with masses of string-like feeding tentacles; phyllodocids are surface-dwelling, crawling worms with leaflike feelers or 'cirri'; the various kinds of mantis shrimp that inhabit the reef are all vigorous predators; decapod shrimps, with their five pairs of legs, abound in a great variety of sizes and colours; the ram's horn shell is a cuttlefish that inhabits deeper waters off the reef.

*P*hotographed from below, these corals, on a reef slope not far from the surface, create a beautiful 'reef garden', alive with vivid and brilliantly contrasted colours. Conditions close to the surface often promote the growth of hardy, stunted forms of species that in deeper situations can occur in branched forms.

A huge solitary coral, showing its limestone skeleton and central mouth. The tentacles have been retracted; when they are extended, they convey worms and other small animals to the mouth. Solitary corals are so called because, unlike most corals, they do not form colonies, existing as large single polyps that sit on the reef but remain unattached.

Below

*D*uring the day the polyps of this bubble coral (*Plerogyra sinuosa*) resemble a bunch of submarine and delicately patterned grapes. Each of the bubbles of this species of hard coral consists of a rounded limestone skeleton covered with tissue. At night the tentacles come out, extending between the bubbles to take in nutrients.

*T*he soft coral *Sarcophyton trocheliophorium* can radically alter its appearance by expanding or retracting its polyps. When the polyps are retracted as a result of a disturbance the coral takes on a bare, sculpted look that is in sharp contrast to the flowery appearance it has when fully expanded. Soft corals lack the solid central skeleton of the hard corals and thus are not reef-builders.

A school of large batfish (*Platax orbicularis*), distinguishable by their bluish grey colour, flat bodies and small rounded mouths, photographed near Heron Island. Juvenile batfish often deceive potential predators by floating on the surface and presenting the appearance of dead leaves.

Below

*T*he black coral, *Cirrhipathes anguinus*, forms slender whip-like stems which wave freely in the current. Black corals, which usually occur at considerable depths, can also grow as intricately branched and spreading shapes. While the skeletons are black, the tiny six-tentacled polyps that cover them — not visible in this photograph — can range from yellow to dull grey.

Right

*T*his red sea fan, growing at right-angles to the current, is well placed to catch passing plankton. Like most gorgonians, sea fans favour positions in the shelter of ledges.

*T*he blue angel fish (*Pomacanthus semicirculatus*) has blue-fringed fins and tail, luminous blue body markings and eye patch and bright blue spots. It is the most prolific of several species of beautifully marked and similarly flat-bodied angel fish that frequent the coral reefs.

Willandra Lakes

Willandra Lakes

<small>P</small>ink cockatoos (*Cacatua leadbeateri*) inhabit most of the inland of Australia.

Previous pages
<small>L</small>ow shrubs are the most conspicuous form of vegetation in the Willandra region.

*T*he greater long-eared bat
(*Nyctophilus timoriensis*) is a
comparatively rare species. It hunts
nocturnally for beetles, moths and
tree-dwelling insects.

A male and female red kangaroo (*Macropus rufus*). Red kangaroos are the largest of the Australian marsupials. They are widespread throughout central Australia and extend into the western part of the eastern states. Despite their common name, most female red kangaroos are bluish grey in colour and grey males also occur. Females are also appreciably smaller than males.

*K*angaroos on a saltbush plain. This part of New South Wales is near the eastern extremity of the western grey's range. The eastern grey does not extend into Willandra, but the red kangaroo and the common wallaroo are two other large marsupials that graze on the area's grass and shrub vegetation.

The earthbound but fleetfooted emu (*Dromaius novaehollandiae*), standing as high as two metres, is Australia's largest and the world's second largest bird. It ranges over most of continental Australia, in areas where human habitation is sparse, feeding on grasses, plants and insects. Temporary pair-bonding is a characteristic of emu behaviour and couples will often travel long distances together. The sexes are hard to tell apart, but the female can be distinguished by the darker patch of blue skin at the top of the neck.

Emu chicks, with their striped brown and white down and spotted heads, are considerably more strikingly coloured than the adults. Even though they are able to move around and feed almost immediately after hatching, the chicks remain in the care of the male adult which shelters them beneath his feathers at night for as long as eighteen months. As a result the adult can be precluded for almost two years from further breeding activity.

Left

A patch of grass close to trees or bushes, like the nitre-bush (*Nitraria billardieri*) shown here, is a typical setting for the nest in which emus lay the large eggs which were once eagerly sought as ornaments. Emus usually lay about ten eggs in a clutch. These are incubated for about eight weeks by the male, which also rears the chicks when they are hatched.

*I*ts drooping branches, rough bark
and long slender leaves highlighted
by the rising sun, and its roots
brutally exposed as a result of soil
erosion, this berrigan (*Pittosporum
phylliraeoides*) is one of the few trees
that can grow in the sands of the
Willandra Lakes. An inland species,
berrigan can grow as a shrub or as a
substantial tree that reaches a height
of ten metres.

Below

*B*errigan produces yellowy orange fruit capsules, less than two centimetres long, which open to reveal succulent-looking glutinous red seeds. Despite their appearance, however, these seeds are poisonous to humans although Aborigines crushed them and used the paste as linament for muscular soreness. Warmed berrigan leaves were placed on the breasts of mothers with newborn infants to stimulate the flow of milk.

A paddymelon plant spreads like a net over part of a dune. This species, introduced from South Africa, is a member of the cucumber family, to which pumpkins and melons also belong. The plant produces rounded hair-covered green fruit that turn yellow as they ripen. In the middle of the picture is a spindly nitre-bush (*Nitraria billardieri*), a species that occurs in sandy areas and clay soils throughout the continent, and behind are the ubiquitous bluebushes.

*T*he red-capped robin (*Petroica goodenovii*) typically perches on a branch as it surveys the ground, often with seeming nonchalance, for insects and worms. It is predominantly an inhabitant of drier inland areas but ranges widely over all but the very northern part of the continent. The female is less brightly coloured than the male, its brown plumage creating a less striking contrast. The small cup-shaped nest, built in the branches of trees or shrubs, is often pirated by cuckoos, which lay their eggs there for the unsuspecting robins to hatch.

*A*mong the taller forms of vegetation in the Willandra Lakes region are the rosewood (*Heterodendrum oleifolium*), seen here on the right with its roots exposed by erosion, and the white cypress pine (*Callitris glaucophylla*), growing in a small cluster on the left. Although the white cypress pine, a non-flowering species, can grow to twenty metres in some locations, it does not usually exceed about ten metres in the more arid areas.

A female fat-tailed dunnart (*Sminthopsis crassicaudata*) carries several members of her litter on her back. Because the fat-tailed dunnart is able to utilise fat stored in its tail, and obtains all the moisture it needs from the insects that constitute its staple diet, it is well suited to survive in even the most arid regions of the continent. Nevertheless, it is more plentiful in areas where higher rainfall results in an abundance of insects.

Below

*B*urton's snake-lizard (*Lialis burtonis*) is one of a number of Australian lizards that, because they lack legs, are commonly mistaken for snakes. These legless lizards are predominantly outback dwellers, although Burton's snake-lizard is to be found in a variety of habitats.

Above

The presence of ants or termites is sufficient to qualify almost any area of Australia as a habitat for the short-beaked echidna (*Tachyglossus aculeatus*), one of Australia's two egg-laying mammals, or monotremes. This spine-covered furred animal uses its long, sticky tongue to reach into ant and termite nests, or disturbs the nest with its snout or forepaws and then gathers up its prey from the ground around the nest.

Right

Many caterpillars are covered with prickly hairs that can cause irritation to anyone who handles the insect. Caterpillars feed on a wide range of vegetation. What the caterpillar eats must to a large extent sustain the adult butterfly which feeds abstemiously on nectar and sap.

The saltbushes (*Sclerolaena* spp.) that, together with a variety of native grasses, dominate the ridges of the Chibnalwood Lakes, near the southern extremity of the region, are typical of the region's lunette and lakebed vegetation.

*I*n the Willandra Lakes region, as in most other parts of Australia, the fox (*Vulpes vulpes*) poses a significant threat to much of the native wildlife. This voracious carnivore, which in winter feeds also on fruits and insects, was introduced into Victoria in the middle of last century to satisfy the whims of hunting enthusiasts. It has since spread through most of continental Australia and has adapted to a wide range of habitats.

*M*ore destructive than any other introduced animal, the European rabbit (*Orocyolagus cuniculus*) defeated all attempts to control its inexorable spread until the introduction of myxomatosis checked its increase. In semiarid areas the number of rabbits is determined largely by rainfall.

Another introduced animal that has proved versatile in its adaptation to most Australian environments, except for the extremes of wet and dry, is the feral goat (*Capra hircus*), a grazing animal which has ravaged the plantlife of numerous regions and provided unwanted competition for many species of native animals.

*W*ith a liking for open grasslands and a taste for crops and introduced plants, the crested pigeon (*Ocyphaps lophotes*) has been able to capitalise on the clearing of large tracts of land for farming. It is now distributed widely over the inland of Australia.

*T*he chestnut quail-thrush (*Cinclosoma castanotum*) derives its name from the chestnut patch on the lower part of its back. It frequents the semiarid regions of southeastern Australia and extends into the desert areas of the centre and west where its chestnut colouration becomes more extensive to blend with the predominant yellow-brown of the environment. It is a ground feeder on insects and the seeds of plants. While foraging for food it moves rapidly back and forth in a circular pattern.

Mulga parrots (*Psephotus varius*) are widespread throughout the inland parts of southern Australia. This photograph shows the marked difference between the male and the female. The bright green of the male, offset by vivid flashes of yellow and orange, stands out strongly against the relatively dull tones and much less striking colour contrasts that characterise the female.

Western and
Central Tasmania

Western and Central Tasmania

*T*he ferocious teeth and jaws of the Tasmanian devil (*Sarcophilus harrisii*).

Previous pages

*T*he autumnal colours of the deciduous beech (*Nothofagus gunnii*)
contrast with the deep green of native conifers and the spiky foliage
of the grass tree (*Richea pandanifolia*).

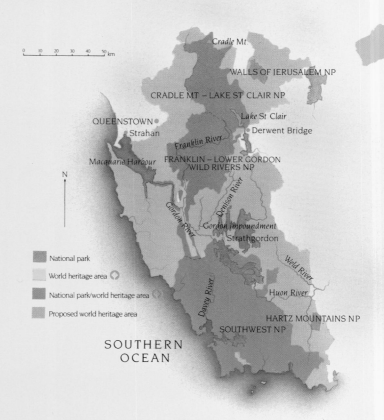

oth central and southwest Tasmania display a great variety of landscapes which in turn support vegetation types of spectacular diversity.
The area's vegetation mirrors both the climatic changes that have
occurred over the past 18 000 years and the effects of human habitation.

The sedgelands that are a feature of both the coastal area and the Central
Plateau are remnants of the tundra that characterised most of the region at
the height of the last ice age. The now extensive cool temperate rainforests
— isolated to a few pockets in the cold period — spread as a result of the
gradual warming of the climate between 10 000 and 5000 years ago. During
the last 5000 years the area covered by rainforest has been considerably
reduced by the effects of bushfires, some of them caused by natural phenom-
ena, but many more the result of burning by Aborigines. The much more fire-
tolerant sedgeland and eucalypt gradually came to dominate the rainforest
edges and western spurs and slopes, destroyed by fire as it spread uphill from
the buttongrass plains.

The rainforest, most abundant in the area of the lower Gordon and
Franklin rivers, is characterised by myrtle beech and sassafras, but also contains three conifers endemic to Tasmania: the famous Huon pine, the celery
top pine and the King Billy pine. In other lowland areas tea-tree and bauera
predominate, while the buttongrass is the dominant vegetation of the
sedgelands. At higher levels stunted trees are much more in evidence and on
the open moors above 1000 metres the apparent barrenness is belied by the
richness of the heath vegetation.

While many of the common Australian marsupials are found in this area,
it is in the lakes that the region's most distinctive fauna is contained. In these
remote habitats live several primitive forms of crustacea, known as syncarids,
that survive nowhere else in the world.

Among the abundant birdlife of this part of Tasmania the most important species is the endangered orange-bellied parrot, which now breeds only
in the sedgelands near and to the south of Macquarie Harbour.

This detail shows the cypress-like leaves and the reddish pollen-cones of a Huon pine (*Lagarostrobos* [*Dacrydium*] *franklinii*), an endemic Tasmanian rainforest species noted for its great longevity and slow growth. A century and a half of exploitation for furniture manufacture and boatbuilding has greatly reduced the distribution of this distinctive Tasmanian conifer.

The nectar from the white flowers of the large leatherwood tree (*Eucryphia lucida*) yields the much sought after leatherwood honey. A Tasmanian endemic, leatherwood is confined to lowlands and areas of medium altitude where rainfall is high and fire rare. *Eucryphia* is the sole genus of the plant family Eucryphiacene and consists of two species in southern Chile, two in Tasmania and one in mainland southeastern Australia.

The bright green leaves and crimson blooms of the climbing heath (*Prionotes cerinthoides*) stand out in brilliant relief against the rough bark of a rainforest tree in southwest Tasmania. The genus is endemic to Tasmania and is confined to the wet areas of the west and southwest. Its closest relative in the Epacrid family is the south Chilean *Lebatanthus*.

Right

A Huon pine, typically ragged in appearance, grows beside the Gordon River in southwest Tasmania's Wild Rivers National Park. The Huon pine has a predilection for riverside locations — although it will grow well away from rivers, especially on protected slopes — and if the planned flooding of the Gordon River had not been aborted in 1983 valuable stands of these ancient trees would have been irrevocably lost.

An adult common wombat (*Vombatus ursinus*) with its young at the entrance to a burrow. One of the most familiar and widespread of Australian marsupials, this burrowing herbivore is more numerous in Tasmania than on the mainland. It feeds nocturnally on grasses and plant roots, which it digs up with powerful claws. The female produces one young at a time which remains protected in the pouch for about six months.

A male and female Bennett's wallaby (*Macropus rufogriseus*) in typically open woodland in the Cradle Mountain area. These wallabies are easily identifiable by the reddish brown patch on their necks. The species abounds throughout eastern and southeastern Australia but the Tasmanian animals are distinguished by their shaggier fur, slightly darker colouration and by a much more limited breeding period.

Smaller and more lithe than the spotted-tailed quoll, the eastern quoll (*Dasyurus viverrinus*), once widespread in the southeast of the mainland, is now confined to Tasmania. It inhabits dry sclerophyll forest and is most commonly found near the edges of eucalypt areas.

Caught here in a characteristic show of aggression, the spotted-tailed quoll (*Dasyurus maculatus*) is reputedly one of the most ferocious of Australian predators. Its prey, which it typically attacks from behind, include small mammals, birds, snakes and lizards. The quoll is found in all parts of Tasmania and is widely distributed on the eastern mainland.

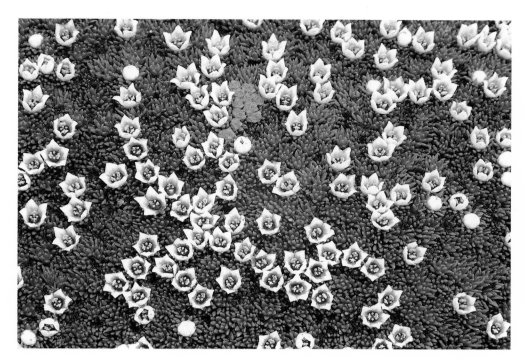

Far left and left

*I*n the Tasmanian alpine regions are a number of cushion plants that are not found in an identical form anywhere else in the world. On the far left an expanse of cushion plant covers a plateau in front of Lot's Wife and Mount Weldon in the southern highlands. Although from a distance they resemble thick carpet, these plants really consist of minuscule and tightly knit branches. At left snow cushion (*Donatia novaezelandiae*) is pictured in bloom in the Cradle Mountain area.

*I*n spring and summer these thick, glossy leaves of the native laurel (*Anopterus glandulosus*) will be adorned with large white or pink flowers. This plant grows in moist eucalypt and temperate rainforests at altitudes below 1000 metres. It is most commonly a shrub that grows to about three metres.

*T*he red, upright blooms of the prickly-leaved scoparia (*Richea scoparia*) bring many a Tasmanian mountainside spectacularly to life during December and January. This endemic plant, common to the alpine regions of Tasmania, withstands cold and strong winds and can cover large areas with densely matted bushes.

105

The colour differentiation between the male and female Australian fur seal (*Arctocephalus pusillus doriferus*) is obvious in this photograph. The much darker male is also larger and can grow up to two and a half metres long. These marine mammals, once threatened by the depredations of the sealing industry, are restricted to the waters around the southeast of the continent and the coasts of Tasmania where they are found in isolated colonies, such as the one south of Maatsuyker Island.

Among the Tasmanian fauna of greatest scientific significance are a number of species of syncarids — primitive forms of crustacea — that are found in the mountain lakes of the Central Plateau. These lakes are the only region in the world where the Tasmanian mountain shrimp or anaspides (*Anaspides tasmaniae*) survives as a living creature. Elsewhere it is known only as an ancient fossil.

Above

A land crayfish (*Parastacoides tasmanicus*) at the entrance to its burrow in the Southwest National Park. This species is endemic to Tasmania and is common throughout the slopes, swamps and plains of the southwest where it inhabits mainly still-water environments.

*T*he Burrow's tree frog (*Litoria burrowsi*), which grows to five centimetres in length, is endemic to Tasmania. It occurs frequently in rainforests and can be identified by the peculiar quacking sound it emits and by the golden patches on its back. It lays its eggs on grasses and other vegetation in still water.

A profusion of man ferns (*Dicksonia antarctica*), all sending out new fronds, thrive in the moist conditions along the banks of the Weld River. This tree-fern species is widely distributed throughout cooler areas of mainland southeastern Australia but is most abundant and luxuriant in southern Tasmania.

A towering and venerable myrtle beech (*Nothofagus cunninghamii*) plays host to numerous epiphytic mosses in a southwestern rainforest. Myrtle beech is the dominant species in many rainforest areas throughout the state, especially at lower altitudes. Rather less imposing examples of the species also grow in the understorey of eucalypt forests and in alpine regions it can exist as a large shrub.

Right

*A*nother tall rainforest tree is the sassafras (*Atherosperma moschatum*) which shares dominance of many temperate rainforests with the myrtle beech. Here epiphytic mosses cover the twisted trunk and spreading roots of a sassafras in the Cradle Mountain –Lake St Clair National Park.

The little pygmy possum (*Cercartetus nanus*) feeds on the nectar and pollen of numerous flowers, as well as insects, that occur in its varied habitats. It ranges through forests and heathlands in the east and southeast of the mainland and Tasmania.

Characteristic of the Tasmanian pademelon (*Thylogale billardierii*) are its short snout and red-tinged fur. Also typical is its fondness for the grassy verges of forests. Once common on the southeastern tip of the mainland, this small macropod is now confined to Tasmania and the Bass Strait islands.

Left

The Tasmanian bettong (*Bettongia gaimardi*), a nocturnal feeder on fungi and other plantlife, spends the days resting in its grassy nest. Although 200 years ago it was found as far north as southern Queensland, it now exists only in eastern and central Tasmania.

Right

A tiny sugar glider (*Petaurus breviceps*) clings tenaciously to a slender branch as it peers into the blackness. During its nocturnal foraging for the native fruit, saps and flowers that, along with insects, constitute its diet it glides noiselessly between trees, covering up to fifty metres in a single leap. It is kept airborne by the flap of skin that stretches parachute-like between its extended paws and feet. The sugar glider is commonly found in many of the mainland and Tasmanian forests.

Previous pages

The curse of bushwalkers when it occurs in the form shown in this photograph, taken in the Cradle Mountain–Lake St Clair National Park, the famed horizontal scrub (*Anodopetalum biglandulosum*) is more often a leaning rather than strictly horizontal tree. It is endemic to Tasmania where it grows predominantly in moist areas of the south and southwest.

The Tasmanian cave spider (*Hickmania troglodytes*) is among the most primitive of living spiders. Caves are one of the many moist and covered places in which it finds a congenial habitat. These spiders also live under rocks and tree roots where they build permanent horizontal webs parallel to the ground and attached to cave walls and other vertical surfaces. The spider lurks under this web and pulls through insects that fall on top of it. It is distinguishable by yellow marks on the underside of the abdomen.

The bright-eyed brown butterfly (*Heteronympha cordace*) can be found above 900 metres in the mountains of New South Wales, the Australian Capital Territory, eastern Victoria· and Tasmania. At night the larvae feed on sedge (*Carex* spp.). Like most butterflies, the adults are diurnal.

The striking-looking Tasmanian masked owl (*Tyto novaehollandiae castanops*) is more commonly encountered than its comparatively rare mainland counterpart from which it is distinguished by its larger size and generally darker colouration. Like all barn owls it frequents caves, but it forsakes these dark hideaways during the night to fly through forests and even over open country.

*A*n endangered species, the orange-bellied parrot (*Neophema chrysogaster*) is known to breed only in a restricted area in southwest Tasmania although it ranges into the coastal areas of South Australia and Victoria. It is notable for the strange buzzing sound it makes when disturbed and by its clumsily irregular flight pattern.

*S*hining white trunks are the hallmark of the swamp gum (*Eucalyptus regnans*), known in Victoria as mountain ash. This species, which is exceeded in height only by the coniferous Californian redwoods, grows frequently to seventy metres and occasionally, as here, to more than ninety metres. The tree in the centre of this picture, taken in the Styx valley in southwest Tasmania, is reputed to be the tallest hardwood in the world.

*T*he characteristically rough-barked pencil pine (*Athrotaxis cupressoides*), pictured at left, and the long-lived King Billy pine (*A. selaginoides*), shown at right, dominate many of the higher altitude Tasmanian rainforests. These two closely related species are endemic to Tasmania and often combine to form a hybrid species, *A. laxifolia*, which is itself a dominant species in some forests and which in alpine regions can grow as a shrub.

Lord Howe Island

Lord Howe Island

A red-tailed tropicbird (*Phaethon rubricauda*) soars above Lord Howe Island.

Previous pages
*L*ooking south from the northwest tip of the island. In the foreground
are the yellow blooms of *Cassinia tenuifolia*.

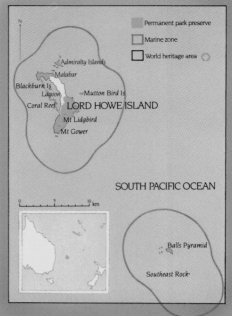

Every year in spring and summer Lord Howe Island and the smaller islands nearby are invaded by myriad seabirds which come to this relatively predator-free haven in order to breed and rear their young. While most of them migrate during the winter, at least two species, the masked booby and the grey ternlet, remain in the area the whole year round. Many of them establish colonies on exposed headlands or on rocky cliff ledges of the offshore islands; others nest in the palm forests that grow on various parts of the island. For the large masked booby Lord Howe is its most southerly breeding ground; for at least two other species it is the chief breeding ground. Numerous species of wading birds are regular visitors but do not breed on Lord Howe.

Humans and introduced animals have taken a heavy toll on the landbird population on the island. Many species of landbirds, including some endemics, are now extinct and one — the endemic and flightless Lord Howe Island woodhen, which was reduced to a small group in the Mt Gower rainforest — has only been saved as a result of a successful breeding program.

Apart from birds, land fauna is restricted to one mammal, a bat, two lizards — which, however, now exist almost exclusively on the smaller islands — and invertebrates, including about a dozen species of butterflies, some spiders and several species of endemic snails that are common in the forests.

The reef that encloses the shallow lagoon on the west of the island is the world's most southerly living coral reef. It supports a range of marine life that, while much less diverse than that of the Great Barrier Reef, is rich and interesting. Rock platforms on the eastern side of the island, particularly at Neds Beach in the northeast, also support an array of marine animals, including areas of colourful coral. Hundreds of species of ocean fish, mainly tropical species, abound in the waters off the island group.

Rainforest vegetation covers much of the island, especially in the moist upland areas. A high proportion of the island's plant species are endemic. Endemic species include several tree ferns and mountain palms, the screw pine, with its long, stilt-like prop roots and the remarkable spreading banyan with its aerial roots. Although few of them create spectacular splashes of colour, there are almost 200 species of flowering plants, and just under one-third of them are endemic.

Left
The coral reef on the western side of
Lord Howe Island is the most
southerly in the world. Here a diver
swims over a branching, tree-like
mass of gorgonian coral.

Previous pages
The branches of the banyan (*Ficus
macrophylla* ssp. *columnaris*) sprout
roots that eventually form new trunks.
This subspecies of Moreton Bay fig is
endemic to the island. In the
understorey is the thatch or kentia
palm (*Howea forsteriana*).

Although trevallies (*Caranx* sp.) are offshore fish, large schools are sometimes encountered close to the reef where they follow and prey on schools of smaller fish. Along with such species as bluefish, salmon, garfish and perch, they are sought after by anglers in the waters around Lord Howe Island.

*T*he conspicuous angel fish (*Chaetodontoplus conspicillatus*) is one of the numerous flamboyantly coloured fish that frequent the reef. It presents an arresting sight, with its uniformly dark body contrasting starkly with the luminous blue fringe and the striking, but subtly blended, markings of its face and tail.

Left
*T*his xenia coral (*Xenia elongata*), its tentacles extended and waving in the current, was photographed three metres below the surface in Erscotts Hole, in the lagoon near the edge of the coral reef.

One of several endemic species of tree ferns (*Cyathea* sp.) that grow in the mountainous regions in the south of Lord Howe Island.

*H*umid and wet conditions in the mountainous areas account for the large numbers of rainforest species that proliferate there. The big mountain palm (*Hedyscepe canterburyana*), shown (*left*) in flower on Mt Gower, can grow up to ten metres high, emerging from the surrounding vegetation. Thick fern and palm vegetation (*below*) dominates large areas of the slopes of Mt Lidgbird.

Permanently moist conditions support a rich 'cloud forest' on the summit of Mt Gower (*above*), with tree trunks clothed in mosses, liverworts and ferns. Until very recently this relatively inaccessible area was the last remaining habitat for the woodhen (*Tricholimnas sylvestris*), which had fallen victim to the predations of humans and introduced animals. Another rare endemic species that frequents the forest floor leaf litter is the snail *Gudeoconcha sophiae* (*below*).

Faced with extinction, the flightless woodhen was bred in captivity in the early 1980s and then released in various parts of the island.

127

*T*wo birds common in the lowland areas are (*right*) the Lord Howe Island golden whistler (*Pachycephala pectoralis contempta*) and the green-winged pigeon (*Chalcophaps indica*). Both birds appear unafraid of humans and are readily visible in the lowland forests.

*A*nother easily observed bird on Lord Howe Island, between September and May, is the flesh-footed shearwater (*Puffinus carneipes*), named for the fleshy pink colouring of its legs and feet. It lives in large colonies in the lowland palm forests on the east of the island where it nests in burrows in the soil. During the winter it migrates to more northerly warmer climes, moving as far afield as the waters around Japan.

*L*ike some species of native birds on Lord Howe, the two lizards that existed naturally on the island — the gecko *Phyllodactylus guentheri*, pictured here, and the skink *Leilopisma lichenigerum* — were hunted almost to extinction by the exotic animals brought by humans. Cats and rats in particular were responsible for the destruction of these small reptiles. Both species are occasionally to be seen in the rocky lowland areas, but are more numerous on Balls Pyramid and the other islets.

A longicorn beetle, one of the thousand species of Australian long-horned beetles. These beetles are usually slender-bodied with antennae that turn on a series of ball-joints. Their larvae feed on living plants.

*S*ophora howinsula

*M*oorei orchid (*Dendrobium moorei*)

*M*ountain daisy (*Olearia ballii*)

*M*ountain rose (*Metrosideros nervulosa*)

*L*ordhowea insularis

*L*ord Howe tea tree (*Melaleuca howeana*)

*L*ord Howe Island can boast almost 200 species of native flowering plants, of which almost one-third are endemic. All the plants shown on this page are endemic to the island. While most of the island's plants provide only discreet patches of colour that do little to distract from the predominant greenness of the vegetation, a number of them, including *Sophora howinsula*, mountain daisy and mountain rose, flower profusely. *Sophora howinsula* is a tree that can grow to ten metres; the moorei orchid grows as an epiphyte on tree branches in the southern mountains; the mountain rose is either a small bush in open situations or a substantial tree in the forests; and the mountain daisy is a low shrub growing to less than two metres. *Lordhowea insularis*, a shrub that grows to a maximum height of about two metres in the moist forested areas, is more remarkable for its large, shiny, serrated leaves than for the brilliance of its blooms. The Lord Howe tea tree is usually a low bush that is most conspicuous in exposed rocky and sandy situations.

The pumpkin bush (*Olearia mooneyi*), shown flowering (*top*) on Mt Gower, grows only on the mountaintops. Berrywood (*Ochrosia elliptica*), whose fruit and leaves are shown above, is found mainly in coral sand near beaches. Both the wedding lily and the island apple are endemic Lord Howe species.

Below
*I*sland apple
(*Dysoxylum pachyphyllum*)

*W*edding lily
(*Dietes robinsoniana*)

This beautifully patterned nudibranch (*Chromodoris elizabethina*) belongs to the group of sponge-feeding nudibranchs known as Dorids, which are characterised by the cluster of gills in the anal region.

This reef wall, displaying a variety of corals, sea stars and green algae, was photographed twenty metres below the surface near Noddy Island in the Admiralty Island group.

Far right

Although they resemble corals and have a similar structure, anemones do not have a skeleton. They use their stinging tentacles to paralyse the marine animals on which they feed.

The red-mouthed stromb (*Strombus luhuanus*), with its bright red aperture, is conspicuous on the sandy shallows.

The black stripe which passes over the eye of the black-backed butterfly fish (*Chaetodon melannotus*) serves as an effective decoy, helping to confuse potential predators and causing them often to attack the tail instead of the head. The black patch on the back expands and the yellows deepen at night to provide further camouflage.

Among the most effectively camouflaged of all the reef fish are the various species of scorpion fish, including the one shown here, the pugnacious-looking Cook's scorpion fish (*Scorpaena cookii*). Similar in looks and behaviour to the stonefish, but with much less deadly spines, scorpion fish are wily predators.

One of the largest fish in the waters around coral reefs is the grotesque-looking hump-headed wrasse (*Coris bulbifrons*) which can grow to almost two metres long.

Right
The clown fish (*Amphiprion akindynos*), with its distinctive broad white stripes, stays close to the tentacles of sea anemones.

*F*rom below, the sooty tern (*Sterna fuscata*), seen here hovering high above its breeding grounds, appears almost entirely white. Its head and the upper parts of its wings and tail are, however, black. Of all the birds that nest on Lord Howe, this one does so in the greatest numbers. Although their main food consists of small marine animals, scooped from on or just below the surface, sooty terns on Lord Howe are frequently seen catching cicadas in mid-flight.

*R*ed-tailed tropicbirds (*Phaethon rubricauda*) on Lord Howe Island are distinguished by a light pink tinge that is absent from the plumage of their more northerly counterparts. These large and imposing seabirds breed prolifically in their nesting sites on exposed cliff ledges. The chicks retain their fluffy grey plumage for less than six weeks before they assume their white adult feathers. At just over three months they can fly and dive quite proficiently.

Left
*L*ord Howe and its surrounding islands provide the world's most southerly breeding grounds for the masked booby (*Sula dacytlatra*), a seabird usually associated with more tropical locations. The exposed situation shown here, on Roach Island, is a typical nesting site for these birds, which build their nests out of debris in shallow depressions in the ground.

The plants growing here in moist forest on the slopes of Mt Lidgbird include the fitzgeraldii (*Dracophyllum fitzgeraldii*), the spiky-leaved tree in the foreground, tree ferns (*Cyathea* sp.) and the mountain rose (*Metrosideros nervulosa*).

Right

The bright luminous green of still unfolding fronds contrasts with the darker flat green of the older ones in this epiphytic fern (*Blechnum* sp.) growing in the moist forest on Mt Gower. These ferns, several species of which grow on Lord Howe Island, are sometimes called 'water ferns'.

Right

In most mainland locations, screw pines have stilt roots less than about a metre in length, or no stilt roots at all. The endemic Lord Howe species (*Pandanus forsteri*) is a particularly tall species and has stilt roots often five metres long. In the most spectacular example, on the Boat Harbour track (*bottom*), these 'props' are as long as eight metres.

New South Wales
Rainforests

New South Wales Rainforests

*T*he southern angle-headed dragon (*Gonocephalus spinipes*), a wet forest species.

Previous pages
*T*wo subtropical rainforest plants: the sword-leaved plant (*Helmholtzia glaberrima*)
and the low herb, *Elatostema reticulatum*.

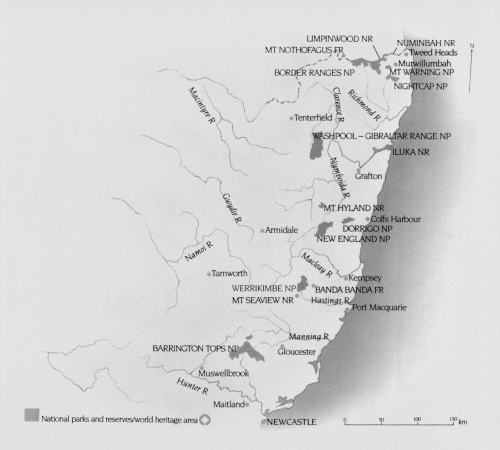

The canopies of rainforests are formed usually by medium to large trees that, in one or more strata, dominate the rest of the vegetation. Although some species are common to more than one rainforest type, each of the four kinds of rainforest found in northern New South Wales has its own distinctive vegetation pattern.

Subtropical rainforests have the greatest diversity of trees in their canopies. A common dominant in these forests is the large conifer, the hoop pine. Black bean trees, with their brilliant displays of blooms, and strangler figs are among the most distinctive tree species in subtropical rainforests. Coachwoods are the large trees most characteristic of warm temperate rainforests, sometimes sharing their supremacy with other species such as sassafras and lillypilly, while in the cool temperate rainforests of northern New South Wales the most important, and often the only, dominant tree is the Antarctic beech. In dry rainforests hoop pines, or the deciduous lace bark, often overtop other canopy trees. A very widespread rainforest tree in the state is the towering brush box, found in all except cool temperate rainforests.

Commonly found looping below the canopy, especially in subtropical and dry rainforests, are many species of thick-stemmed vines and, in subtropical rainforests particularly, epiphytic ferns and orchids are abundant. In the understorey, in all but dry rainforests, ground and tree ferns, as well as palms, provide a lushness that is accentuated by the rich green of mosses. The floor of dry rainforests is usually more sparsely vegetated with low, prickly shrubs.

Of the rainforest fauna, birds are perhaps the most numerous and varied. The fruits of many of the canopy trees, the rich insect life of the leaf litter and the absence of many of the predators that occur in more open environments contribute to a large bird population. Among the species that are particularly associated with these rainforests are the green catbird — a relative of the bowerbirds — and the superb and Albert's lyrebirds, the latter being endemic to the Queensland–New South Wales border area.

Except for a blacker variety which occurs in some northern New South Wales rainforests, the mountain brushtail possum (*Trichosurus caninus*) is a uniform grey colour throughout its range. It inhabits rainforests and open forests in coastal areas from south Queensland to southern Victoria.

Right

Typically rich understorey vegetation of a cool temperate rainforest in the Dorrigo National Park. Tree ferns (*Cyathea leichhardtiana*) thrive in this moist environment, as do epiphytes, including the elkhorn (*Platycerium bifurcatum*) in the centre.

The most familiar of all Australian ringtails, the common ringtail possum (*Pseudocheirus peregrinus*) ranges widely throughout eastern Australia. Those found in northern New South Wales and southern Queensland rainforests form a subspecies (*P. p. pulcher*), often popularly called rufous ringtails.

Although they are more common in open grassy areas rufous bettongs (*Aeprymnus rufescens*) thrive in the warm temperate rainforests where there is an absence of feral predators. These small macropods are noted for their noisy and aggressive courting behaviour.

*B*rush box (*Lophostemon confertus*) is a prominent species on the margins of northern New South Wales rainforests. Popular as a street tree in towns, in its natural setting it is a majestic tree that can grow to more than forty metres tall with girth of almost two metres. It produces white feathery flowers.

Right
*R*ainforest trees produce a variety of blooms, many of them colourful and delicate. While many rainforest species bloom discreetly, the flowers of the black bean and the lace bark, both large trees prominent in drier rainforests, are abundant and conspicuous.

Black bean (*Castanospermum australe*)

Sassafras (*Doryphora sassafras*)

Walking-stick palm (*Linospadix monostachya*)

Lace bark (*Brachychiton discolor*)

Lillypilly (*Acmena smithii*)

Plum pine (*Podocarpus elatus*)

*S*uperb lyrebirds (*Menura novaehollandiae*) are restricted to the moist forests of eastern Australia from south Queensland to Victoria. These unusual birds are skilled mimics and indefatigable singers, incorporating in their songs snatches of other birds' calls. The most elaborate songs, accompanied by dancing, are presented by the males when, with their tail feathers raised in elaborate display, and standing on their specially constructed mounds, they perform their spectacular courtship rituals.

*A*lbert's lyrebird (*Menura alberti*) is found only, and even then rarely, in subtropical rainforests in the far north of New South Wales and the extreme south of Queensland. Slightly smaller and darker than the superb lyrebird, and more shy of humans, Albert's lyrebird is in other ways similar to its more familiar relative. Although the male's tail feathers are less elaborate, the courtship display is just as imposing. This photograph shows a female with a chick. With both lyrebird species the female alone builds the nest — a dome of sticks and other debris — incubates the single egg that is laid, and rears the young.

The strikingly contrasted and partly iridescent colours of the noisy pitta (*Pitta versicolor*) often seem dimmed by the obscure light of many rainforest settings. This small bird is more often heard — it has a loud three-note whistle — than seen. It is a ground dweller and builds a lined dome-like nest of sticks, bark and roots. Its eats worms and insects, but is especially partial to snails.

Male brush turkeys (*Alectura lathami*) construct large incubation mounds which, as they are added to year after year, often grow to about two metres high. Decaying leaf and other organic matter causes the temperature inside the mound to rise, creating conditions favourable for the incubation of the twenty or so eggs that are laid, buried in the mound and then left to hatch.

The north coast green tree frog (*Litoria chloris*) is recognisable by its regular and clearly differentiated ventral and dorsal colouration and by its bulging, orange-ringed eyes. It lives mainly in the rainforests of northern New South Wales and in pockets of rainforest in Queensland.

The green and golden bell frog (*Litoria aurea*) is common along the coast of New South Wales and Victoria where it lives in permanent still water. It is unusual among frogs in that it does not catch insects, but preys instead on other frogs and even small snakes. It hunts mainly at night, often among bulrushes that grow at the edge of its watery habitat.

*F*letcher's forest frog (*Lechriodus fletcheri*) is basically a rainforest species which breeds in pools and small puddles and becomes evident only after rain. Its predominantly brown colour, flecked sometimes with green, and barred rear limbs, provide excellent camouflage, allowing the frog to blend easily with the leaf litter on the forest floor.

In Willowie Scrub in the Washpool National Park is the state's largest stand of coachwood (*Ceratopetalum apetalum*). These large trees, with their characteristically mottled trunks, dominate the canopy of many of the warm temperate rainforests, which are also characterised, as here, by a fairly sparse understorey.

Ficus watkinsiana, seen here in the early stages of its growth, is the most common of several species of strangler figs that grow in the subtropical rainforests of northern New South Wales. These figs grow around their host trees, eventually killing them.

Right

The booyong (*Argyrodendron* sp.), seen here in the foreground, often dominates subtropical rainforests. Other common features of these forests are the thick vines, or lianes, that wind around the trunks of large trees and the bird's nest ferns (*Asplenium australasicum*) that grow as epiphytes on their trunks.

Right

The smooth trunks of a stand of brush box trees (*Lophostemon confertus*) in Dorrigo National Park. The trunk of a brush box tree can, with age, achieve a diameter of two metres. One venerable specimen, in Terania Creek, is reputed to be 1200 years old.

The green catbird (*Ailuroedus crassirostris*) seldom ventures from its rainforest habitat, where it is easily recognised by the cat-like wailing sound that both sexes use to proclaim their territory. Catbirds belong to a group of bowerbirds whose bower consists of patches of ground strewn with leaves, but whose courtship display consists usually of a chase between branches of trees. Unlike other bowerbirds, catbirds form permanent pair bondings and the male helps to rear the chicks. Cup-shaped nests of twigs, leaves and vines are built in trees. They eat mainly fruit and leaves but will also eat animals and small birds.

The red-browed finch (*Aegintha temporalis*) is one of only two Australian species of finch that regularly occur in rainforests. The red-browed finch is common along the whole of the continent's east coast and generally prefers the edges rather than interiors of closed forests.

As part of a mating ritual, a male satin bowerbird (*Ptilonorhynchus violaceus*) displays one of the blue objects he has arranged around his bower. If a female is responsive to his display, which involves dancing and mimic-like calls, the two birds will quickly mate and the female will be driven away. Females are a greyish green colour.

*A*dult male king parrots (*Alisteris scapularis*) acquire their superb orange-red head and breast plumage only when they are about thirty months old. Until then they have the less distinctive green head and breast of the female. In rainforests these birds tend to remain out of sight, high in the canopy.

*W*onga pigeons (*Leucosarcia melanoleuca*) live in a wide variety of forest environments along the coastal region of eastern Australia. Reluctant fliers, these squat grey birds feed on fruits, leaves and insects that they find on the ground. Their numbers have been greatly reduced since European settlement, partly through the clearing of forests, but also because they were extensively hunted as a pest to crops and, occasionally, as a source of food. Unlike other pigeons, the male wonga pigeon performs an elaborate, highly rhythmic courtship dance.

*L*iving mainly on the edges of the rainforest, the brown pigeon (*Macropygia amboinensis*) is distinguishable from other pigeons by its brown colour and by its unusually long tail. Although it has been extensively hunted and much of its habitat cleared, this pigeon has adapted well to human incursions by developing a taste for the seeds and fruits of introduced plants.

*F*reshwater crayfish are fairly common throughout moist areas of Australia, inhabiting a variety of still and moving water environments and often burrowing into the muddy banks of streams. They feed mainly on rotting vegetation, which is in plentiful supply in many rainforest locations, as well as on the flesh of dead animals. This Mt Lewis crayfish, its claws raised in a show of aggression, is one of numerous species of the genus *Euastacus*, which are restricted to the eastern side of the continent and frequent streams in hilly or mountainous regions. These species are characterised by spiny bodies and often by bright colours.

*F*reshwater crayfish lay eggs which hatch to produce large numbers of tiny offspring, or larvae, which are effectively fully formed miniature adults. These larvae cluster on the underside of the parent's abdomen, hanging on by their pincer-like claws until they become independent. Among the cluster of crayfish larvae shown here are a number of flatworms, or planarians.

Mastiff-bats are named for the prominent jowls which are a feature of most species. They are also characterised by the length of their tails. Of the six Australian mastiff-bats, the eastern little mastiff-bat (*Mormopterus norfolkensis*) has the narrowest distribution, being restricted to a coastal strip of New South Wales and southern Queensland. Its species name derives from a mistaken belief that this bat occurred on Norfolk Island.

The crescent of gold that surrounds its head and extends on to its back is the feature for which the golden-crowned snake (*Cacophis squamulosus*) is named. This attractive snake is found along the east central coast. Its bite is venomous but rarely harmful to humans.

Despite its popular name, the flowers of the pink rock orchid (*Dendrobium kingianum*) vary greatly in colour. They can range from deep mauve to white, although the latter is uncommon. Clusters of these orchid plants often appear on tree branches and cliff faces throughout its range — from the north coast of New South Wales to southern Queensland.

Right
This strangler fig (*Ficus watkinsiana*) has completely enveloped its host tree and is now established in its own right as a subtropical rainforest giant, complete with epiphytic ferns (*Platycerium superbum*) and clinging vines. In the foreground are the leaves of a black bean.

Long spikes of flowers are produced by the king orchid (*Dendrobium speciosum* var. *hillii*) which grows epiphytically on rainforest trees. Another variety of this species is the rock lily. It grows on rocks and has slightly larger and more strongly scented flowers.

Northern New South Wales is the southern limit of the range of the fawn-footed melomys (*Melomys cervinipes*), a native rodent. It is predominantly a rainforest dweller which feeds on the ground and in tree branches on leaves and fruit, as well as on insects and small mammals. It builds its nest of grass or leaves in the branches of trees.

Snails, like this one (*Helicarion* sp.), and other invertebrates play an important role in the rainforest ecosystem by helping to break down the leaf litter, rotting wood and other organic matter on the forest floor. They are in turn preyed upon by many birds.

Although the bush rat (*Rattus fuscipes*) is the most numerous of Australia's bush rats, it is elusive and rarely sighted. It lives in a variety of habitats but thrives particularly in areas, such as rainforest understoreys, where there is a thick ground cover. It forages nocturnally, mainly for insects but, if these for some reason are in short supply, it will feed on fungi or other vegetable matter. Four distinct subspecies are distributed widely around the eastern and southern coasts and the far southwest of the continent.

*M*oist forest conditions have proved very congenial to a wide variety of butterflies and moths. Moths, being the hardier of the two, have also adapted quite well to many more arid environments. These photographs show two specimens of the genus *Antheraea*, which includes many of the well-known emperor moths. The furry bodies and feather-like antennae that characterise all emperor moths can be seen in these photographs. Also visible, though much more conspicuously in the specimen below (*Antheraea janetta*), are the round markings, or 'eye spots', on the wings.

One of only two pademelon species that now exist on the Australian continent, the red-necked pademelon (*Thylogale thetis*) is the more restricted in its distribution, inhabiting rainforests and other moist forests along the southern Queensland and New South Wales coastal strip. These small, timid macropods — they grow only to half a metre tall — typically inhabit the forest verges, sheltering in the forest cover during the day and emerging at night to graze on adjoining grasslands.

The parma wallaby (*Macropus parma*), thought to have become extinct in the early 1930s, was rediscovered in 1966. Its sparse distribution, along the north and central coast of New South Wales, and its daytime occupation of rainforests and other forests, may account for its apparent disappearance. This small wallaby grows to about half a metre long and can be distinguished by its white throat, chest and belly.

The long-nosed potoroo (*Potorous tridactylus*) is restricted to coastal areas of high rainfall. It stays under cover, finding its food — which includes fungi and insects — among the leaves and in the soil.

Right
A scene on the banks of Rosewood Creek, in Dorrigo National Park, showing aspects of the understorey vegetation of a warm temperate rainforest. The tall trees with dappled trunks are coachwoods, which typically dominate this type of forest. Numerous tree ferns (*Cyathea* sp.) are in evidence and on the ground is a range of ferns, grass-like plants, shrubs and herbs. Over the fallen log in the foreground is growing the creeping herb, *Elatostema reticulatum*.

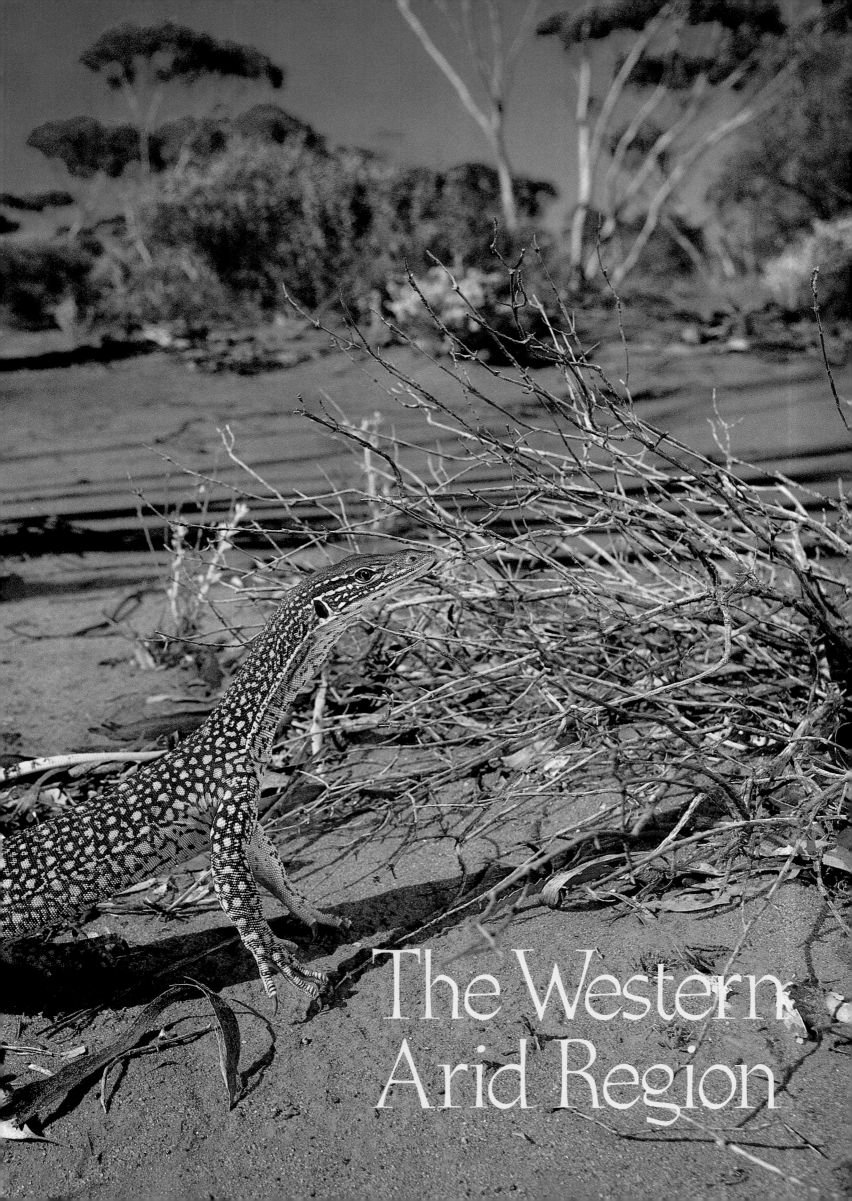

The Western
Arid Region

The Western Arid Region

*D*esert blooms illuminated by the burnished glow of a central sunset.

Previous pages
A Gould's goanna and tall mulla-mulla in the red loam of the western desert.

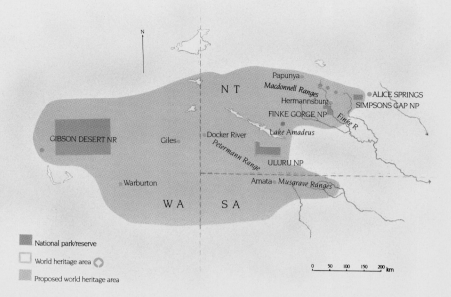

National park/reserve

World heritage area

Proposed world heritage area

0 50 100 150 200 km

The western arid region, which takes in most of central Australia, includes a number of quite distinct flora and fauna habitats. While much of region consists of deserts which are characterised by sandplains and dunes, and sometimes salt lakes, there are, especially in the mountain ranges, moister pockets that support a considerable range of vegetation and some distinctive species of fauna including a number of frogs.

It is on the spinifex-covered arid plains that much of the region's most characteristic and abundant fauna is to be found, for this area provides a habitat for the most diverse reptile population in the world. Whereas many species of mammals have disappeared from this area in the last 200 years, lizards of all types — geckos, dragons, goannas and skinks — continue to thrive in a great range of forms and sizes, and snakes, though rarely sighted, are common throughout the region.

While much of the desert is covered with spinifex and other grasses, often surprising splashes of colour are provided after rain by numerous flowering plants that have adapted to the conditions. These include many species of daisies as well as grevilleas, hibiscus, peas — including the famous Sturt's desert pea. Among the larger species are acacias and some eucalypts. River red gums and coolibahs grow along watercourses in some parts and bloodwoods and desert oaks relieve the otherwise stunted vegetation on many of the sandplains.

In the Finke Gorge National Park in the Macdonnell Ranges grows a distinctive palm, *Livistona mariae*, which depends on the water that is constantly available there. This palm is a survivor of times when moist conditions prevailed more generally. Another relict species is the cycad, *Macrozamia macdonnellii*, restricted to shaded valleys in the Macdonnell and Harts ranges.

Most of the mammals in the western arid region are small, nocturnal creatures, including a number of native rodents and many smaller marsupials. Their incidence has been reduced by the presence of feral animals such as cats, foxes and rabbits. Larger mammals include the ubiquitous red kangaroo, the common wallaroo and, in the ranges, several species of rock wallabies.

In spring and summer the spotted emu bush (*Eremophila maculata*) bears tubular flowers, spotted on the inside, which vary in colour between lemon yellow and bright red. There is great variation in size; this shrub can stand just over half a metre tall or can grow to a height of three metres.

Hakea is an endemic Australian genus which has more than 120 species scattered throughout the continent. About ten of these are found in the western arid region and their flowers range in colour from white to pink. This is *H. eyreana*, a bushy shrub which can grow as tall as seven metres.

*S*turt's desert pea (*Clianthus formosus*), pictured here amid a sea of leafy burr-daisies (*Calotis latiuscula*), is the floral emblem of South Australia, but its large dark red flowers with their black patches at the centre enliven the central Australian landscape after spring rains.

Right
*S*tanding out against the scrubby vegetation surrounding Uluru are the golden pine-like blooms of a flame grevillea (*Grevillea eriostachya*). This fine-leaved shrub grows to about three metres tall on the sandplains and dunes of central Australia. One of only ten species of *Grevillea* that grow in the arid interior, the flame grevillea also thrives in areas of higher rainfall and richer soil.

The blend of tones that distinguish this black-footed rock wallaby (*Petrogale lateralis*) reflects the colours of the rocky outcrops which are its natural habitat. Although this species occurs in several areas in central and southwestern Australia, the Macdonnell Ranges population is distinctive and forms a separate race.

Below

The highly venomous, but attractively patterned, desert death adder (*Acanthophus pyrrhus*), which grows to about three-quarters of a metre long, is closely related to the widely feared common death adder. It is a desert dweller which closely mirrors the colours of its environment. This snake generally spends its days hidden in the sand or sheltering under clumps of grass and emerges at night. It attracts birds, mammals and small reptiles by convulsing the narrow tip of its tail.

Far right

Enough soil has been built up in the ridges and depressions of this imposing and beautifully moulded rockface to support a variety of vegetation types. Straggling eucalypts, shrubs, bushes and a number of grasses provide a range of greens that contrast effectively with the rich golden brown of the rock. Decomposing leaves and other vegetation from these plants help build up the soil deposits, which are further nourished by the rains that wash down the rock surface.

168

Unlike most parrots, the mulga parrot (*Psephotus varius*) has a sweet mellow call. When disturbed while foraging on the ground for seeds, berries and grasses, this bird removes itself to a nearby tree where it calmly awaits its chance to return. Mulga parrots, usually seen in pairs or small groups, are widespread throughout the drier inland areas of the southern part of the continent. The bird shown here is a male; the female has similar, but less vivid, colouration.

A familiar but nonetheless impressive sight in arid and semiarid parts of the continent, especially soon after dawn and approaching dusk, is large flocks of budgerigars (*Melopsittacus undulatus*) swarming across the sky in search of water or grass seeds. These small green and yellow parrots, so familiar in captivity, are in the wild swift-flying, free-wheeling nomads whose movements display a remarkable degree of coordination.

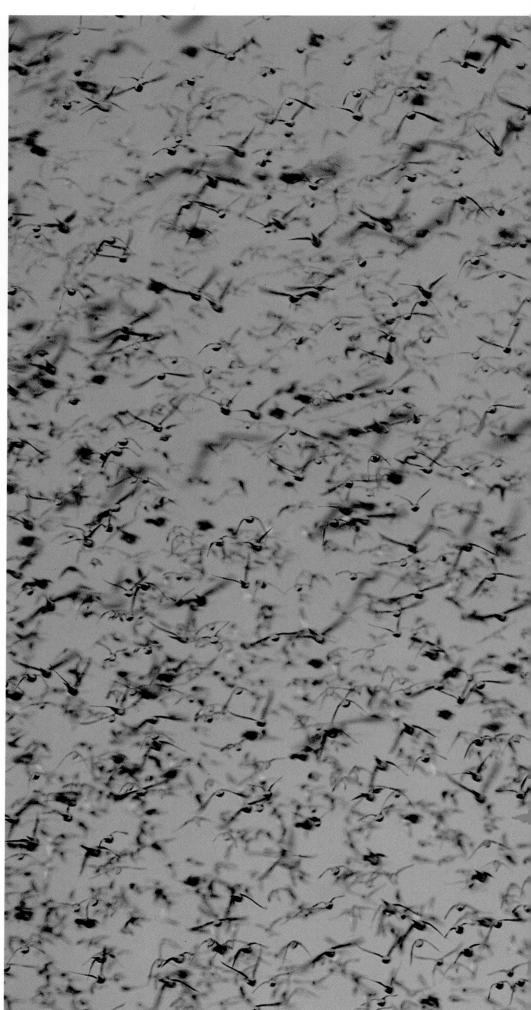

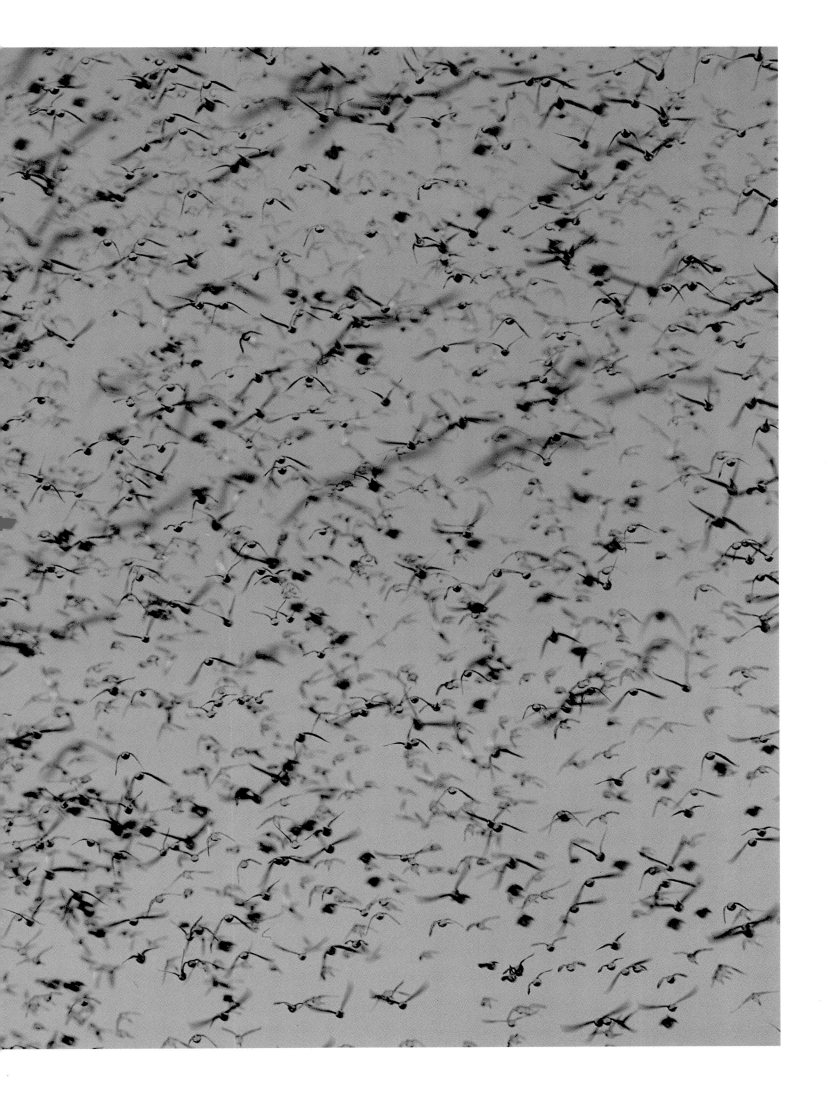

Rocks are the preferred habitat of the spiny knob-tailed gecko (*Nephrurus asper*), whose smooth head and spine-covered body contribute to its generally grotesque appearance. When disturbed this gecko rises up to adopt the threatening stance shown here.

Short-horned grasshoppers (family Acrididae) are common throughout arid areas and vary greatly in form and colour. Many, like the almost perfectly camouflaged insect shown here, have large wings and are good fliers; others are flightless and have only vestigial wings or none at all.

Probably the most ancient of Australian dragons, the thorny devil (*Moloch horridus*) is a creature of the western and central deserts. Despite its grotesque appearance and fearsome mien, it is thoroughly harmless, except to the small black ants which it grinds between its flat-topped teeth and devours in enormous quantities. It grows only to about fifteen centimetres long and moves slowly, in an awkward waddling motion, on its thin, weak legs. A complex arrangement of spiky scales make up its protective armour.

The Petermann Range is one of the numerous rocky ranges that are among the conspicuous landmarks of central Australia. In much of the range the vegetation is sparse and stunted, with the occasional exception of a lone eucalypt, its grey-white trunk and branches standing out against the brown of the rock and muted green of the grasses.

A stand of desert oak (*Allocasuarina decaisneana*), with an understorey of *Acacia* and other shrubs, in the Petermann Range. These rough-barked trees, which grow to about fifteen metres tall, have very fine branchlets that hang limply from the widely spreading branches. The saplings have smooth trunks and branches and appear quite different from the fully grown tree. This species is found, more typically than here, in open sandy country.

Right

A solitary cabbage palm (*Livistona mariae*) in Palm Valley in the Finke River gorge. This relict species, which is endemic to a small area around the Finke River where it cuts through to the Macdonnell Ranges, is a survivor of the times when lush moist forests covered this part of the continent. The shiny green, fan-like leaves that cluster at the top of the tapering bare trunk as much as twenty metres above the ground contrast vividly with the predominant brown of the landscape.

*E*merging at night from the deep burrow in which it shelters from the heat of the day, the spinifex hopping mouse (*Notomys alexis*) forages for insects, seeds and other plant matter. This small long-tailed rodent performs feats of considerable dexterity, constantly changing direction as it hops rapidly about on two or four legs.

*T*his rare close-up shows details of the snout, mouth and claws of the marsupial mole (*Notoryctes typhlops*). This minuscule burrower in desert sands grows to only about ten centimetres long. It is completely blind, with only vestiges of eyes beneath the skin, and has no external ears. It lives on insects and the larvae of beetles.

*T*he varied but uniformly stunted vegetation growing around Mt Conner includes the yellow burr-daisy (*Calotis latiuscula*), the cotton-like white blooms of tangled mulla-mulla (*Ptilotus latifolius*), cattlebush (*Trochodesma zeylanicum*) in the middle foreground and a number of grasses, including spinifex.

176

Left

Perched, typically, on a dead tree branch, the brown falcon (*Falco berigora*) watches, ready to swoop on any small reptiles, mammals and insects that it spots on the ground. The brown falcon is distributed throughout the continent and Tasmania, and extends into New Guinea.

Right

Against a background of spinifex, a mulgara (*Dasycercus cristicauda*) devours a plague locust. This small plump marsupial, distinguished by its black-crested tail, is a vigorous nocturnal hunter of insects and other small animals, from which it obtains most of the moisture it needs. The mulgara inhabits desert regions of central and southern Australia where it lives in sometimes multi-tunnelled burrows which it digs in the sand.

The general creamy fawn colouration of the western blue-tongued lizard (*Tiliqua occipitalis*) is offset by the bands of darker brown across its back and tail and, more strongly, by the black stripe that runs backward from each eye. It is common in the more southerly parts of the arid inland.

Crested pigeons (*Ocyphaps lophotes*) are primarily birds of the inland, preferring lightly wooded locations to more densely vegetated ones. In central Australia they are most often found near watercourses or in the vicinity of dams or billabongs. Their liking for the seeds of a wide range of plants and crops has allowed them to spread into coastal regions and into areas that have been cleared for agriculture.

Top left

Pandorea, a genus of woody shrubs and rainforest lianes, grows in all Australian states and on all parts of the mainland except the western third. Of the four Australian species, however, only the spearwood bush (*P. doratoxylon*), which in spring produces masses of cream, red-throated, bell-shaped flowers, grows in the arid centre.

Above left

The small, crimson berry-like fruit of the ruby saltbush (*Enchylaena tomentosa*), one of more than 150 species of saltbushes that thrive in the dry conditions and saline soils of outback Australia, stand out in striking relief against the drab grey-green of its leaves.

Top right

One of the most delicately coloured of all Australian wildflowers is Sturt's desert rose (*Gossypium sturtianum*), whose large mauve flowers with crimson centres bloom in arid outback areas between later winter and early summer.

Above right

Clusters of large flowers sprout at the end of the erect metre-long stems of the tall yellowtop (*Senecio magnificus*). This perennial daisy is one of the most widespread of the nine *Senecio* species found in the arid centre.

*I*t is hardly surprising that the vertical
fluffy blooms that characterise most
species of *Ptilotus* have attracted such
popular names as lambstails,
pussytails, feathertails and
bottlewashers. *P. exaltatus*,
photographed here in the Petermann
Range, is known variously as
pussytail and tall mulla-mulla. It is
one of many species of *Ptilotus* that
grow in drier parts of the continent.

*A*n inhabitant of rocky outcrops in the desert areas of central Australia, the perentie (*Varanus giganteus*), with its bluey grey and brown colouration and yellow spots, can blend imperceptibly into its surroundings. Growing to more than two metres long, the perentie, one of the goannas or monitors, is the largest lizard in Australia and the second largest in the world. Its diet includes mammals, birds and smaller reptiles.

Geckos are small lizards with soft, thin skin covered with protective scales. Sometimes, as in the case of the knob-tailed gecko (*Nephrurus wheeleri*), these scales are in the form of thorny tubercles. Although they will drink water where it is available, geckos generally obtain the moisture they require from the insects that almost exclusively form their diet. They are nocturnal animals, and in the dark their pupils, which appear as small slits in daylight conditions, expand to fill the whole eye.

Many geckos of the genus *Oedura* have colour patterns that blend with the environment in which they are found. Some, like this one, have digits which are dilated at the ends and under which are sticky pads or claws that can be extended or retracted.

Although there are various species of eucalypt in Australia's desert areas, they are more dependent than some other plants on the presence of subsoil moisture and often occur along watercourses. Riverbeds, riverbanks and the rocky beds of gullies are the favoured habitats of the river red gum (*Eucalyptus camaldulensis*), a handsome tree whose smooth white bark is patterned with random patches of grey or red. In favourable conditions it can grow to forty metres high.

Right

*B*loodwood (*Eucalyptus terminalis*), named for the reddish colour of the sap that exudes from its trunk, grows only to about ten metres. It is a rough-barked tree with thick foliage and blooms in winter with a profusion of white flowers. It is often found in the vicinity of rock masses such as Uluru, where it benefits from the large amount of water that runs off the surface after rain.

*D*espite its appearance, *Macrozamia macdonnellii* is not a true palm; it is a cycad. It is a relic of times when rainfall was much higher and temperatures less extreme, and grows only in relatively moist and shaded areas of the Macdonnell Ranges. Its large fronds, with their thin, spiky leaves, sprout at the top of a trunk, most of which grows beneath the ground. The plant produces brown cones, some of which are visible here, but does not flower.

The Wet Tropics

The Wet Tropics

A Herbert River ringtail (*Pseudocheirus herbertensis*) and its young.

Previous pages
*F*loating leaves of a nardoo (*Marsilea* sp.), an aquatic fern.

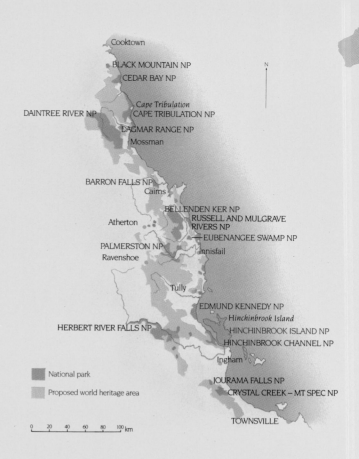

Cooktown
BLACK MOUNTAIN NP
CEDAR BAY NP
Cape Tribulation
DAINTREE RIVER NP   CAPE TRIBULATION NP
DAGMAR RANGE NP
Mossman
BARRON FALLS NP
Cairns
BELLENDEN KER NP
RUSSELL AND MULGRAVE
Atherton   RIVERS NP
EUBENANGEE SWAMP NP
PALMERSTON NP
Innisfail
Ravenshoe
Tully
EDMUND KENNEDY NP
Hinchinbrook Island
HINCHINBROOK ISLAND NP
HERBERT RIVER FALLS NP   HINCHINBROOK CHANNEL NP
Ingham
National park   JOURAMA FALLS NP
Proposed world heritage area   CRYSTAL CREEK – MT SPEC NP
TOWNSVILLE
0 20 40 60 80 100 km

Although tropical rainforests dominate most of the wet tropics and contain its most distinctive vegetation species, the area encompasses a number of other types of forests. There are, for example, areas of dry sclerophyll forest, stands of paperbark as well as more open savannah woodland. In the estuaries of some of the rivers are significant mangrove forests. Within the rainforests are small patches atypically dominated by fan palms, and in parts of the area where rainforests descend to the sea, stands of sheoaks often feature prominently along the beaches. Within the rainforests themselves at least thirteen types of vegetation pattern have been described. What perhaps most clearly distinguishes the wet tropics from the vegetation of most tropical areas is its almost universal lushness, the result of significant falls of rain during the dry season and, in the upland regions, the effect of constant mist and cloud cover.

The wet tropics is wonderfully rich in fauna, and although much of this is shared with other regions, there are many endemic species. Ten per cent of the almost 130 species of birds known in the area are endemic and another 10 per cent are visitors that are found nowhere else in Australia. Others are shared exclusively with the adjoining Cape York region. Rainforests provide a haven for many smaller mammals and among the wet tropics endemics are several that are restricted to very specific localities. One of these is the Thornton Peak melomys, found only in the area after which it is named; another is a white subspecies of the lemuroid ringtail possum.

Butterflies are the most conspicuous of the invertebrates and often rival the birds in the brilliance of their colours. Some larger species from a distance are easily mistaken for birds. The many rivers, creeks and lagoons in the region provide habitats for numerous species of frogs, including many endemic and restricted species, as well as for some reptiles. The reptilian population of the region is particularly large and encompasses numerous tropical rainforest specialists.

*R*ed lacewing butterfly (*Cethosia cydippe chrysippe*)

*L*acewing butterfly (*Cethosia cydippe*)

*C*airns birdwing (*Ornithoptera priamus euphorion*)

*M*ountain blue butterfly (*Papilio ulysses*)

*B*utterflies abound in the tropical rainforests and more than half the known Australian species of butterflies are found there. The butterflies shown here are among the most colourful species and the mountain blue butterfly, the bright metallic blue of its upper wing surface contrasting with the brown underneath, creates a dazzling flashing effect when it flies. The mountain blue and the birdwings are among the largest of butterflies and, when flying at considerable height, are easily mistaken for birds.

The Cairns birdwing is the largest
butterfly in Australia and one of the
largest in the world. The female's
wingspan can be as much as twenty
centimetres and that of the more
brightly coloured male, shown here
on the right, can reach to seventeen.
It is rarely seen outside its rainforest
environment.

*F*lightless like the emu, and only slightly shorter, the southern cassowary (*Casuarius casuarius*) is a bird of the tropical rainforests. The female lays her clutch of eggs in a nest of leaves on the forest floor and leaves the male to incubate them and rear the chicks.

*T*he golden bowerbird (*Prionodura newtoniana*) is an endemic wet tropics species, inhabiting high-altitude areas of the Atherton Tableland. It is the only Australian bowerbird to build a maypole. This consists of two structures of twigs around adjacent tree trunks. Between the trees and close to the ground a branch serves as a platform for the male's courting ritual. White flowers are often used to decorate the bower.

*T*he Australian fern wren (*Crateroscelis gutturalis*) is a tiny ground dweller that prefers the deeply shaded areas of the rainforest. Its subdued tones contrast strikingly with the brilliance of much tropical birdlife. This one is standing on its nest — a domed construction on the ground, built mainly of moss.

Left
*B*uff-breasted paradise kingfishers (*Tanysiptera sylvia*) breed in the north Queensland rainforests for about five months a year — from November to April. The rest of the time they spend in New Guinea. These small, brilliant birds nest in termite mounds, using their bills to create deep tunnels.

A pungent-smelling little animal, the striped possum (*Dactylopsila trivirgata*) lives in sparse populations in forested areas in far northeastern Queensland, as well as in New Guinea. Its natural diffidence and nocturnal habits mean that it is rarely encountered by humans. Most of its diet consists of insects. It finds these in trees, which it climbs with great agility, or in fallen logs.

The Thornton Peak melomys (*Melomys hadrourus*), found only in the vicinity of Thornton Peak in the Daintree, is the largest and rarest Australian member of its genus.

Right

Like the Thornton Peak melomys, the Daintree River subspecies of the darker-coloured Herbert River ringtail (*Pseudocheirus herbertensis cinereus*) is restricted to the Daintree region, where it eats the leaves of rainforest trees.

*L*emuroid ringtail possums (*Hemibelideus lemuroides*) are restricted to a small area of rainforest in northeastern Queensland. Normally they are a brownish grey colour, but in the Carbine Tablelands there is a population that includes a number of rare white possums, like the one shown in this photograph. Lemuroid ringtails are most common at higher altitudes, but the white form is only ever encountered at altitudes of more than 1100 metres. These possums are nocturnal, emerging from the hollows of tree trunks early in the evening to feed high in the branches on leaves, fruits and flowers.

*O*f the two species of tree kangaroo found in the wet tropics, Lumholtz's tree kangaroo (*Dendrolagus lumholtzi*), shown here feeding on leaves, is the more specialised in its habitat. While the slightly larger Bennett's tree kangaroo (*D. bennettianus*) occurs in rainforests at all altitudes, Lumholtz's tree kangaroo is now found only in highland rainforests. This nocturnal macropod sleeps during the day high up in the canopy and at night clambers among branches and up and down trunks eating leaves and fruit. Unlike other macropods, tree kangaroos have quite long forelegs and hind legs that are capable of independent movement. When on the ground they can either walk on all fours or hop in familiar kangaroo fashion. While they are quite adept at climbing trees, they descend backward in awkward movements, finally dropping the last few metres to the ground. Although they are not immediately endangered, both Lumholtz's and Bennett's tree kangaroos have had their habitats reduced by logging and other forest-clearing operations.

195

A green tree frog, *Litoria xanthamera*, photographed at Downey Creek in the Daintree region. This is one of more than twenty-five species of frogs that occur in the wet tropics.

*T*he giant green tree frog (*Litoria infrafrenata*) is distinguished by it size — it grows to fourteen centimetres long and is the largest of all Australian frogs — and by the conspicuous white stripe on its lower jaw. It occurs in coastal parts of Cape York and far northeastern Queensland and feeds mainly on insects, but also occasionally on small mammals. Its fingers and toes have sticky pads which provide security on tree branches but prove an impediment on the ground.

Left

*M*ost frogs of the family Hylidae are climbers rather than burrowers. On the ends of their toes they have discs, under which are sticky pads.

The eastern water dragon
(*Physignathus lesuerii*) never moves far
from water. It is most typically
encountered on branches
overhanging streams, into which it
will drop if disturbed. It can stay
submerged for long periods and
swims very strongly. This lizard,
which can grow to almost a metre
long, ranges all along the east coast of
the continent. The female lays her
eggs in a tunnel burrowed into the
riverbank.

Overleaf
Three species of angle-headed
dragons inhabit the forests along the
central and northern east coast. Boyd's
forest dragon (*Gonocephalus boydii*) is
restricted to the north Queensland
rainforests. Although mainly arboreal,
it lays its eggs in shallow ground
depressions, usually deep in the
forest interior. It grows to more than
half a metre long and is distinguished
by its prominent head spikes and
yellow pouch.

The mangrove hibiscus (*Hibiscus tiliaceus*) flowers in spring and summer in swampy locations along much of the east coast. It is a small tree that grows to about six metres high. Australia's only native rhododendron, the brilliant red *Rhododendron lochiae*, occurs naturally only at high altitudes in north Queensland forests, although it can be cultivated as a garden shrub. In its natural setting it grows two to three metres tall.

Palms dominate the ground vegetation in this part of the rainforest. The tall palms with spreading leaves are fan palms (*Licuala ramsayi*); those growing closer to the ground, as well as higher up, belong to the genus *Calamus*. The epiphyte on the tree trunk at right is the bird's nest fern, *Asplenium nidus*.

Alexandra palms (*Archontophoenix alexandrae*) growing beside a tropical rainforest stream. Alexandra palms, and other tree palms, are well suited to very wet areas where drainage is poor. On the left can be seen a single frond of the fan-palm, *Licuala ramsayi*.

Some of the plants discernible among this dense treetop foliage include the Queensland black palm (*Normanbya normanbyi*), in the lower left centre with deeper green fronds; the basket fern (*Drynaria rigidula*), the epiphyte with the brown sterile fronds at its base; and the golden orchid (*Dendrobium discolor*), hanging below the tree limb in the centre.

Right

The fern fronds growing so profusely in this tangle of vegetation belong to the climbing swamp fern (*Stenochlaena palustris*). In the centre is a frond of a tree fern (*Cyathea* sp.), and on the upper left are the long leaves of a *Pandanus*. In the right foreground can be seen a sapling of the Queensland umbrella tree (*Schefflera actinophylla*).

*P*alm lily (*Cordyline cannifolia*)

*C*luster fig (*Ficus* sp.)

*L*ittle walking-stick palm (*Linospadix minor*)

*G*ympie (*Dendrocnide moroides*)

*F*ruits of four rainforest plants. The hairy leaves of the stinging shrub, or Gympie, which grows on the verges of the forest, can inflict an extremely painful sting. Fruits of the cluster fig were eaten by Aborigines who derived from them moisture, energy and protein.

The fragrant flower of the smooth bolwarra (*Eupomatia laurina*), an ancient and primitive shrub that grows only in rainforests. It belongs to a family (Eupomatiaceae) that has only one other species.

The attractive bright red fruits of the the coral berry (*Rivina humilis*). Coral berry is not a native plant; it is a commonly occurring introduced weed.

The primitive angiosperm, *Idiospermum australiense*, the only species of the family Idiospermaceae, is endemic to the wet tropics. This example, photographed in the vicinity of Noah Creek, clearly shows the plant's seed structure, which is unique among flowering plants. At germination the large seed splits into four large cotyledons, each of which produces a shoot. One of these shoots achieves dominance and can grow into a large rainforest tree. The seed, known locally as 'idiot fruit', is poisonous.

At about the age of two years the blotched yellow colouration of this juvenile green python (*Chondropython viridis*) will change to a more uniform emerald green. This tree-dwelling tropical rainforest species grows to two metres long. It preys nocturnally on small birds and mammals.

When aroused, the brown tree snake (*Boiga irregularis*) can lunge viciously from its branch and inflict a nasty bite on its source of annoyance. This arboreal species ranges across the north coast of the continent and down into New South Wales. It feeds nocturnally on birds, lizards and mammals.

A slaty grey snake (*Stegonotus cucullatus*) devours a small mammal. This species does not usually move far from water and is able both to swim and to climb trees.

An adult female Atherton antechinus (*Antechinus godmani*), a tiny carnivorous marsupial that is restricted to a very limited high-altitude area on the Atherton Tablelands.

The green ring-tailed possum (*Pseudocheirus archeri*) is named for the greenish tint that results from the combination of colours in its coat. This tree-dwelling nocturnal possum lives only in northeast Queensland rainforests where it feeds mainly on leaves, especially those of *Ficus* species.

Right
The black and white Herbert River ringtail (*Pseudocheirus herbertensis*) is slightly more southerly in its distribution than its light-coloured close relative, the subspecies inhabiting the Daintree River. It lives in highland tropical rainforests between the Thornton Peak massif in the north and Ingham in the south. Nocturnally active, it spends its days hidden away in the hollows of trees or in epiphytic ferns.

The Great Sandy Region

The Great Sandy Region

*T*he eastern curlew (*Numenius madagascariensis*) is remarkable for its long curved beak.

Previous pages
*P*alm-like cycads (*Macrozamia miquelii*) grow in this forest on Fraser Island.

Sandy Cape

Platypus Bay   Orchid Beach

GREAT SANDY NP

Fraser Island

Urangan
WOODY ISLAND NP

Mary R
MARYBOROUGH

MAAROOM FHR

Eurong

KAURI CREEK FHR   Inskip Point
                    Rainbow Beach
Tin Can Bay   Wide Bay
TIN CAN INLET FHR   Double Island Point

COOLOOLA NP

GYMPIE

Teewah
NOOSA RIVER FHR

Tewantin

■ National park/reserve

□ Proposed world heritage area

0   10   20   30   40   50 km

In the swampy heathlands of Cooloola lives the ground parrot, a fast-running and elusive terrestrial parrot that is now rare and endangered elsewhere in Australia. In its sanctuary at Cooloola it is relatively safe from the resumption and development of coastal swamplands that has destroyed much of its habitat in other places. Cooloola also plays host to the glossy black cockatoo, another rare and seldom seen parrot which finds in Cooloola's beachfront she-oaks the cones that are its staple diet.

In the great sandy region birds are the most abundant, varied and conspicuous of the fauna. Most obvious are the many seabirds and waders that inhabit or visit the sandy foreshores and the lakes and lagoons. Pelicans are usually in evidence on beaches, as are the less familiar pied oystercatchers and red-capped dotterels; and soaring overhead are likely to be ospreys, Brahminy kites and other marine predators. Often hidden, but claiming attention with their songs and calls, are the many forest and heath inhabitants among which are several rare species.

The swampy and sandy environments are less conducive to the existence of an extensive mammal fauna, although the prevalence of numerous banksias creates favourable conditions for some nectar-eating species such as the Queensland blossom bat and the yellow-bellied glider. The presence of large numbers of dingoes and brumbies on Fraser Island is a heritage of human occupation and exploitation of the area.

Marine fauna is significant, especially in the Great Sandy Strait where extensive mangrove stands and growths of seagrass support populations of turtles, dolphins and dugongs as well as many fish species.

Much of the rainforest on Fraser Island is dominated by satinay, the local species of turpentine, which sometimes shares its pre-eminence with brush box, and kauri and hoop pines. Blackbutts and scribbly gums feature prominently in the patches of sclerophyll forests, while paperbarks typify the taller vegetation of the wallum — the heaths and swamps in deep sands that extend along the southern Queensland coast but are at their most complex and luxuriant in this region.

The white-barked trees in this photograph, taken in a section of swampy forest in the wallum country near Cooloola, are broad-leaved paperbarks (*Melaleuca quinquenervia*). These trees, which thrive in swampy conditions, produce creamy bottlebrush-like blossoms. The tall shrub on the right is the wallum banksia (*Banksia aemula*). Its flowers are a greyish yellow which, as they wither, turn to the orange-brown colour that is evident here. The long spiky leaves in the right foreground belong to a species of grass tree (*Xanthorrhoea fulva*).

The wedding bush (*Ricinocarpos pinifolius*) is named for the profusion of white flowers that it produces in spring. It is found along most of the east coast of Australia where it thrives in sandy soils and exposed locations.

Goat's-foot convolvulus (*Ipomoea pes-caprae*) is a salt-tolerant vine that colonises sand dunes and is common on beaches. It is named for the shape of its leaf, which resembles that of a goat's hoof.

The coast noonflower (*Carpobrotus glaucescens*) is a pigface that grows on dunes and rocks along the east coast. The moisture-laden leaves help sustain the plant in the dry locations in which it often occurs.

Sedges (family Cyperaceae) almost always grow in moist environments. They are usually characterised, like the one shown here on Fraser Island, by narrow, grass-like leaves that grow from underground stems, and they often blossom with a long spiky inflorescence.

*S*crew pines (*Pandanus tectorius*) grow along this stretch of Wyuna Creek on the northeastern side of Fraser Island. This species is most conspicuous on sandy foredunes and is seldom found far from the sea. Sometimes, however, it extends inland for several hundred metres along the sides of creeks.

*A*n ornate rainbow-fish (*Rhadinocentrus ornatus*) in Seary's Creek near Rainbow Beach on Fraser Island. These fish occur along the east coast of Australia in ponds and gently flowing freshwater streams. They are commonly seen in rainforest streams on Fraser, Moreton and Stradbroke islands.

Right
*T*hree epiphytic ferns — a staghorn (*Platycerium superbum*) at top right; an elkhorn (*P. bifurcatum*), further back at top centre; and the profusely spreading fishbone fern (*Nephrolepis cordifolia*) — growing in a Fraser Island rainforest. All three ferns are very common epiphytes in tropical and subtropical rainforests.

*L*arge colonies of crested terns (*Sterna bergii*) breed on Fraser Island, as they do on islands all around the Australian coast. They are swift and graceful fliers and individuals have been recorded as migrating great distances, sometimes travelling the length of the coastline from north to south. Their diet consists almost entirely of fish.

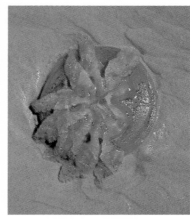

*P*ied oystercatchers (*Haematopus ostralegus*) are among the most familiar of Fraser Island birds. They are seen year round on the beaches, usually in pairs, where they strut about, digging in the sand with their long red beaks for molluscs, worms and other small marine animals. They are also very common on mudflats.

*J*ellyfish (class Scyphozoa), with their translucent texture and delicate colours, can be among the most exquisite of marine animals. Jellyfish are usually bell-shaped animals with thick tentacles which contain stinging cells, or nematocysts. These paralyse prey — mainly small crustaceans — and convey it to the mouth in the centre.

*R*aised high up on its eight pointed legs, the ghost crab (*Ocypode ceratophthalma*) can move at surprising speed across the sand, moving sideways and using only four or six legs at a time. As it runs it frequently stops to make abrupt changes of direction. These crabs live in deep burrows on beaches or in sand dunes.

*O*ctopuses (order Octopoda) are shell-less molluscs with eight tentacles of equal length. Each of these tentacles has a row of adhesive suckers which are used to trap prey, such as fish and crustaceans. When the prey is conveyed to the mouth, it is bitten by the powerful beak-like jaws and, like the prey of a spider, injected with poison before being devoured. Octopuses live in dens, located in rock crevices and usually in shallow water. Octopuses are well camouflaged, and are able to change colour to match their surroundings.

The swift-flowing Wyuna Creek, on the northeastern side of Fraser Island, is here fringed by a thick stand of screw pines (*Pandanus tectorius*), their thick and clustered stilt-like roots emerging from the sandy bottom to support the trunks. Dead leaves from these trees litter the creekbed and hang limply over the trunks and roots.

Right

Satinay (*Syncarpia hillii*) is a turpentine that grows almost exclusively on Fraser Island. It is a tall, rough-barked tree with thick, dark leaves and can grow to more than fifty metres tall. More than any other species it dominates the rainforests on the island. It sometimes shares its dominance with brush box, and the two species also occur in association outside the rainforest. Its timber is extremely durable and the species has been heavily logged. It is particularly useful in marine locations because of its resistance to marine borers.

*P*elicans (*Pelecanus conspicillatus*) are common in freshwater and saltwater environments right around Australia. These large, gregarious birds are usually seen in groups. They use their enormous bills to scoop fish and other aquatic animals out of shallow water. The water that is also scooped up drains out of the large pouch of skin that sags below the bill and the prey is swallowed whole.

*T*he red-capped dotterel (*Charadrius ruficapillus*) is found on Fraser Island all year round.

Gliding silently overhead, a Brahminy kite (*Haliastur indus*) is recognisable by its wing markings and gleaming white head and breast. When it spots a fish or other likely prey it will swoop, grab the victim in its powerful talons and take it away, often to a high perch, to eat.

Pied cormorants (*Phalacrocorax varius*) will dive for their prey, propelling themselves vigorously under the water with their webbed feet moving in unison. They can stay submerged for extended periods. On emerging from the water they will often spread their waterlogged wings to dry, shedding water with the help of oil secreted from their preen glands.

The female rainbow bee-eater
(*Merops ornatus*) can most readily be
distinguished from the male by the
shorter pair of feathers that extends
beyond the end of the tail. These
colourful birds usually avoid forests
and nest in long narrow tunnels in
sandbanks. They are skilled aerialists
and catch their food, which consists
mainly of bees and wasps, while in
flight. They depart all but the far
north of Australia during the winter.

The rare glossy black cockatoo (*Calyptorhynchus lathami*) visits Cooloola to feed on the cones of the casuarinas that grow there. The sombre appearance of the male is relieved only by the bright red of its tail feathers; the female has patches of yellow on its head and neck.

The powerful owl (*Ninox strenua*) dismembers the mammals and birds on which it preys and commonly takes the rear part of an animal back to its roost and there 'stands guard' over it. This roost is usually high above the ground in dense forest. On Fraser Island this large owl is close to the northern limit of its distribution.

A rare, retiring terrestrial and mainly nocturnal bird, the ground parrot (*Pezoporus wallicus*) inhabits coastal heathlands and swamps. It is still common, though not often seen, in Cooloola but has declined in many other places because of the development of coastal land.

A stand of piccabeen palms (*Archontophoenix cunninghamiana*) in the rainforest on Fraser Island. Piccabeens, which can grow to more than thirty metres tall with feather-leaved fronds up to four metres long, are prominent in most subtropical rainforests, particularly beside creeks. They produce pale lilac flowers in pendulous sprays below the bases of the leaves. In rainforests on sand these palms may be more dominant than they are in other rainforests.

A flower from the liane *Tecomanthe hillii*, a rare relative of the wonga vine and restricted to Fraser Island, and a collection of leaves, some of them belonging to satinay, litter the floor of this rainforest.

The rocket frog (*Litoria nasuta*) is one of several frog species that frequent the swampy heaths of Cooloola. It is a swift mover, its speed enhanced by the inordinate length of its legs. This frog is common in the vicinity of still and running water in northern coastal areas from central New South Wales to the Kimberley.

Right

Lace monitors (*Varanus varius*) derive their popular name from the regular and delicate patterning that most of them display. These long and bulky goannas — the largest in Australia after perenties — are agile tree-climbers, especially when disturbed or threatened. They are at home both in trees and on the ground and range widely over non-arid parts of eastern Australia.

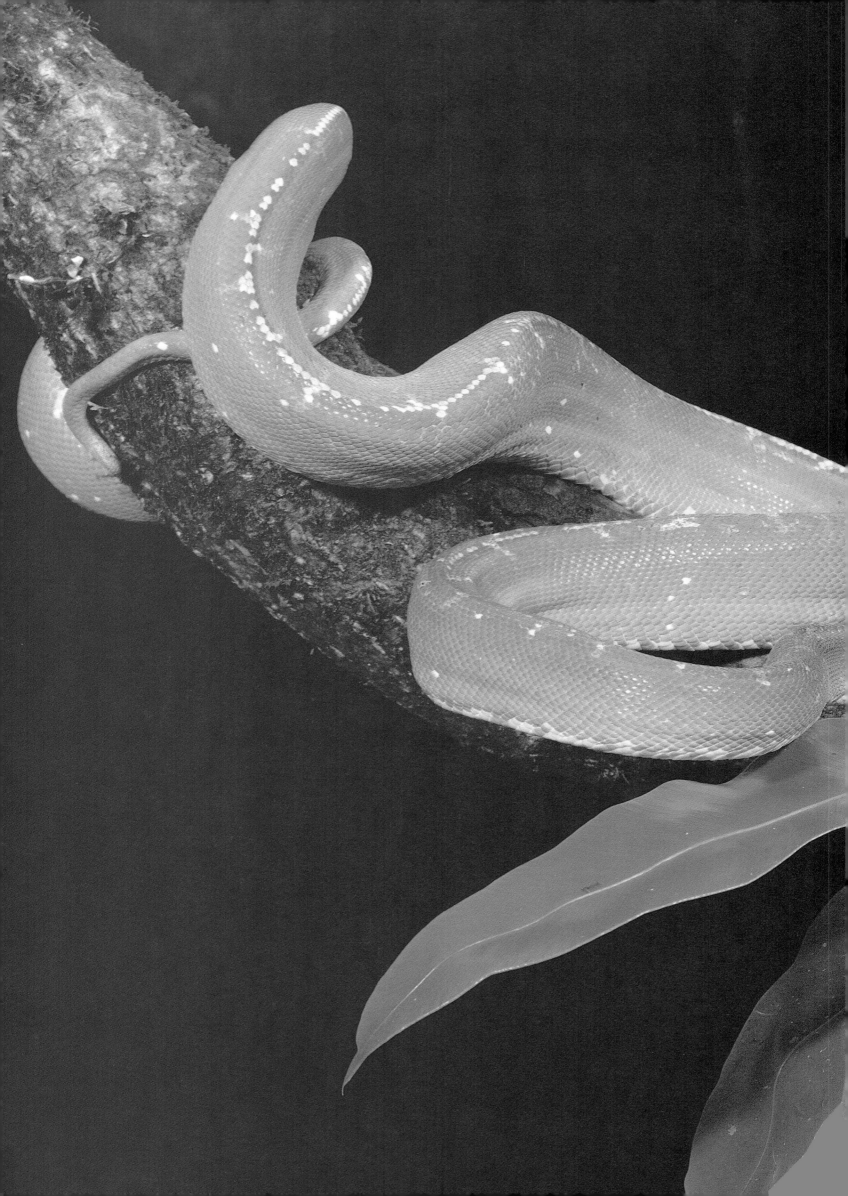

Cape York Peninsula

Cape York Peninsula

*T*he giant tree frog (*Litoria infrafrenata*), Australia's largest native frog.

Previous pages
A green python (*Chondropython viridis*) and an epiphytic bird's nest fern.

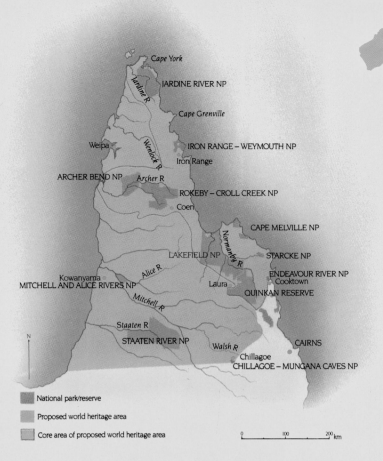

Labels on map:
Cape York
JARDINE RIVER NP
Jardine R
Cape Grenville
Weipa
Wenlock R
IRON RANGE – WEYMOUTH NP
Iron Range
ARCHER BEND NP
Archer R
ROKEBY – CROLL CREEK NP
Coen
CAPE MELVILLE NP
Normanby R
LAKEFIELD NP
STARCKE NP
ENDEAVOUR RIVER NP
Alice R
Cooktown
Kowanyama
Laura
MITCHELL AND ALICE RIVERS NP
QUINKAN RESERVE
Mitchell R
Staaten R
N
STAATEN RIVER NP
Walsh R
CAIRNS
Chillagoe
CHILLAGOE – MUNGANA CAVES NP

National park/reserve
Proposed world heritage area
Core area of proposed world heritage area

0   100   200 km

hile luxuriance is the keynote of the wet tropics to the south, the Cape York region is characterised by a diversity of landscape forms and vegetation patterns that are generally more typical of tropical regions. While most of the peninsula is covered by eucalypt woodlands, limited areas, mainly in the McIlwraith and Iron ranges, are occupied by rainforests. On higher parts of the ranges, these are dominated by hoop pine; in lower areas dominance is shared by many tree species. In gallery forests lining the banks of streams, paperbarks are the most frequent dominants. There are also extensive low-lying wetlands, in some of which the palm *Corypha elata* features prominently, as well as coastal stands of mangroves and expanses of grassy plains and savannah. In the south, near Chillagoe, is an area of limestone country with a distinctive vegetation which includes species of figs and bauhinias.

Much of the fauna in the peninsula is shared with other, and especially tropical, parts of Australia. Most of the seabirds seen around the coasts, and the waders that frequent the lagoons and swamps, are common throughout the north of the continent. Many species in the far northern rainforests also occur in those of the wet tropics as well as in subtropical rainforests.

It is particularly in the rainforests of Cape York, however, that the fauna peculiar to the extreme northeast is to be found. These rainforests also contain the most numerous examples of species that show a continuum between the faunas of New Guinea and Australia. Among the birds in this category are several parrots — the palm cockatoo, Australia's largest parrot; the eclectus and red-cheeked parrots; and the little-understood green-backed honeyeater, an inconspicuous inhabitant of the canopy. Mammals common to the extreme north and New Guinea include the grey and spotted cuscuses and the bare-backed fruit bat, the only cave-roosting Australian fruit bat. The beautiful green python, a rare arboreal snake occasionally encountered in the McIlwraith Range, and confined in Australia to the far northeast, occurs commonly in New Guinea.

Below

*T*he broad-leaved bottle tree (*Brachychiton australis*), photographed here in the karst country near Chillagoe, is an endemic Queensland species that grows especially in fairly arid areas. These large trees are quite fast-growing and can reach heights of more than twenty metres.

*T*hese are the involucres that surround the female flowers and fruit of *Blepharocarya involucrigera*, a large tree found in wet to dry rainforests between Innisfail and Cape York. These involucres, which fall off with the fruit, consist of a ring of sterile inflorescence branches.

Right

*T*he beautiful circular fronds of fan-palms (*Licuala ramsayi*) can reach up to one and a half metres across and create a striking effect when viewed against a clear sky. In some extremely wet lowland areas these palms grow in almost pure stands and in other limited areas they are the dominant vegetation type.

232

*I*n flight the whistling kite (*Haliastur sphenurus*) makes the loud scale-like whistle for which it is named. As it soars, the characteristic bowed shape of its wings is clearly visible.

*I*n Australia the green-backed honeyeater (*Glycichaera fallax*) occurs only in rainforests at the tip of Cape York where it lives high in the canopy.

Right

*T*he male yellow-bellied sunbird (*Nectarinia jugularis*) is distinguished from the female by the iridescent blue-black of its neck. The female's neck, like its breast, is a bright yellow. Australia's only sunbird, this nectar eater is common in north and northeastern Queensland where it frequents the edges rather than the depths of the rainforests.

Far right

*T*he charcoal plumage and scarlet cheeks of the palm cockatoo (*Probosciger aterrimus*), a rainforest bird of the extreme north, combine to create a startling visual effect.

Common in New Guinea, the spotted cuscus (*Phalanger maculatus*) in Australia is restricted to the dense forests at the tip of Cape York. This nocturnal, arboreal animal is distinguished by its very small ears and large, round, red-rimmed eyes.

Conspicuous reddish brown patches around the eyes give this otherwise buff-coloured macropod its popular name. The spectacled hare-wallaby (*Lagorchestes conspicillatus*) occurs across much of northern Australia and is the only one of the four known hare-wallabies to be still secure and widely distributed. This animal is found mainly in open grassland or sparsely wooded areas. It shelters during the day among tall grasses and comes out at night to graze.

The Cape York melomys (*Melomys capensis*) is the extreme northern equivalent of the more southerly fawn-footed melomys, which it closely resembles. It lives in and on the edges of rainforests, and feeds mainly on fallen fruit.

Right

An adult female and young antilopine wallaroo (*Macropus antilopinus*) in typical habitat, at the edge of a forest and near water in the Lakefield National Park. Female antilopine wallaroos generally lack the pronounced tan colouration of the males and they are also significantly smaller.

A brightly coloured looper caterpillar (family Geometridae). These caterpillars are so named because, having three pairs of legs at the front and two pairs at the back of their bodies (and none in the middle), they raise the centre of their bodies into a loop as they move forward. Many colourful moths of the tropical rainforests are adults of these kinds of caterpillars.

An adult dragonfly (order Odonata) emerges from its final shell. After hatching from eggs, dragonfly nymphs remain completely submerged, in either still or slowly flowing water, for just over three months in most tropical locations. During this time they shed more than ten shells. They feed hungrily on tadpoles, mosquito larvae or fish eggs and are preyed upon by fish and frogs, as well as birds and reptiles.

Having shed its final shell, the adult dragonfly begins to fly. Dragonflies are often scintillating insects which are recognisable by their diaphanous wings and straight bodies. These swift fliers normally remain close to water and feed on other insects.

Green tree ants (*Oecophylla smaragdina*) are a tropical species that build a nest of leaves which they bind together with silk produced from their larvae. They fiercely defend these nests by biting intruders and then releasing formic acid on the bite.

The black and red seeds of crabs-eyes (*Abrus precatorius*), seen here lying in their pod on forest leaf litter, are deadly poisonous. This is a widespread and rather weedy species that occurs in tropical regions in Africa, Asia and northern Australia.

Among this collection of leaves and other debris on the floor of a tropical rainforest are the green fruit and withering involucres of a *Blepharocarya* tree and the bright blue fruit of the blue quandong (*Elaeocarpus grandis*).

Like a wad of cottonwool the fruit of the silk cotton tree (*Bombax ceiba*) spills from its fallen pod on to the leaf litter. This deciduous tree occurs in considerable numbers in the rainforest at Lockerbie Scrub.

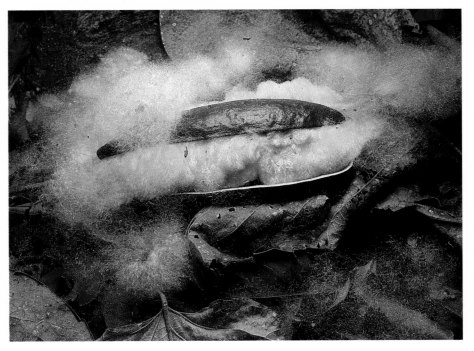

Cocky apple (*Planchonia careya*) is a small tree that occurs in open forests throughout northern Australia. It produces edible fruit and bears these delicate blooms with thread-like crimson and white stamens.

Three stages in the flowering of the lily *Schelhammera multiflora*: the green buds still unopened; a flower coming into bloom; and a fully opened bloom with six petals enclosing the stamens.

Left

The bright red fruit of the red beech, or golden guinea, tree (*Dillenia alata*) opens when mature to reveal its seeds.

The red beech or golden guinea tree is a small tree, common in coastal swampy areas of Queensland's far north. It often grows on beaches. It bears conspicuous, solitary yellow flowers with five broad petals and bright red centres. This one was photographed at Shelburne Bay.

The amethystine python (*Morelia amethystina*) is one of the world's longest snakes — and the longest in Australia. It can grow to over eight metres. It is restricted to northeastern Queensland and occurs in open forests as well as rainforests. Rainforest dwellers, such as the one shown here, are much darker in colour. Despite the slenderness of its body this non-venomous snake sometimes devours large wallabies, as well as birds and smaller mammals.

Left
Agile, arboreal and non-venomous, the common tree snake (*Dendrelaphis punctulatus*) is widespread along the eastern and northern coasts of Australia. Although usually green, its colour varies according to location. This is an example of the dark-coloured varieties that occur in northern Queensland.

The lone Australian species in its family, the wood frog (*Rana daemeli*) is restricted to the Cape York peninsula. It is a ground dweller that occurs in wooded areas, and also in canefields, always close to water. This frog grows to about eight centimetres long and is distinguishable by its conspicuous lateral ridge, large ear covering, or tympanum, and often by lateral warts.

The green tree frog (*Litoria caerulea*) is common in widely differing environments across northern Australia and extends well down into New South Wales.

Below

Male and female wood frogs in amplexus (mating). Very young juveniles have yellow bellies which fade in time to a cream colour.

A freshwater shrimp, one of the aquatic animals that inhabit the rainforest streams of Cape York. This specimen was photographed at Lockerbie Scrub.

A saw-shelled turtle (*Elseya latisternum*) withdraws its head under the protective shell by folding its neck sideways. This turtle is found in east coast rivers from northern New South Wales to Cape York.

A freshwater eel in a rainforest stream at Lockerbie Scrub. Eels are long, slender, sinuous fish which burrow in the sand or mud or hide away during the day in rock crevices. At night they come out to prey on invertebrates and other fish.

*I*ts large size and blotchy wart-covered body, as well as its loud, throbbing mating call, make the cane toad (*Bufo marinus*) hard to mistake. Introduced in 1935 to control one pest, the cane beetle, the cane toad has become a major pest itself by spreading into diverse environments, including rainforests, and preying on native animals.

*T*he purple-crowned pigeon
(*Ptilinopus superbus*) is one of several
beautifully coloured members of its
genus that are found in Cape York.
Unlike the others, however, its
breeding range extends only as far
south as about Proserpine.
Sometimes called the superb fruit
dove, it feeds on more than fifty
different fruiting plants. Its preferred
habitat is lowland rainforest. The
male is the more conspicuous of the
sexes; the female is more uniformly
green and has a smaller crown patch.

*I*ts nocturnal nature and almost total restriction to tropical and subtropical rainforests ensure that the marbled frogmouth (*Podargus ocellatus*) is very rarely seen.

*D*ouble-barred finches (*Poephila bichenovii*), with their characteristic chest bars and strangely hooded appearance, are found in open grasslands throughout most of northern and much of eastern Australia. They are usually in groups, feeding on grass and other plant seeds as well as insects. Their spherical nests, built of grass stems, are entered through a short tunnel and inside are lined with feathers and plant matter. These finches grow to just over ten centimetres long.

The spreading fronds of the large palm, *Corypha elata*, are a common sight in various parts of the Laura Basin. They grow, often in large stands, along the edges of streams in gallery forests; in some areas they are the most conspicuous vegetation type, rising up out of level dry country, as in the photograph above, among a multitude of termite mounds. These palms flower, spectacularly and abundantly, only once before fruiting and dying.

One of the most commonly occurring trees in monsoonal gallery forests in Cape York, and in other parts of northern Australia, is the Leichhardt tree (*Nauclea orientalis*). This rough-barked tree grows to between fifteen and twenty metres and flowers rather diffidently, its lovely orange-centred and white-ringed flowerheads largely hidden by the profusion of new spring leaves. Aborigines made extensive use of this tree: they hollowed out its trunk to make canoes, crushed its seeds and dissolved them in water as a medicine, and ate the fruit as a food. The Leichhardt tree is sometimes popularly referred to as 'canary wood' because of the yellow dye contained in its bark.

While some Torres Strait pigeons (*Ducula spilorrhoa*) remain in Australia for the whole of the year, most migrate between January and March to New Guinea and other more northerly locations, returning in July. They range across coastal northern Australia and extend well down the coast of Queensland, breeding mainly on offshore islands but returning to the mainland to feed exclusively on fruit.

A native of New Guinea as well as Australia, the red-winged parrot (*Aprosmictus erythropterus*) is a bird of the open country and ranges widely over northern and eastern central Australia. In northern Australia it is commonly found among mangroves. It is a leisurely flier that spends most of its day perched in treetops. It feeds on fruit, seeds, blossoms and insects.

Like all but one of the fourteen Australian species of cuckoos, the chestnut-breasted cuckoo (*Cuculus castaneiventris*) lays its eggs parasitically in the nests of other birds. In Australia it is a bird of the Cape York rainforests, but is much more common in New Guinea.

Right

*T*he large flower of a waterlily (*Nymphaea gigantea*), with its subtly variegated petals and bright stamens.

Below

*R*ed flowers of the freshwater mangrove (*Barringtonia acutangula*), a tropical swamp tree. Aborigines used the sap of this tree to poison fish. They also used the bark to stain water; this disturbed the fish, making them easier to catch.

*W*aterlilies grow widely in still, fresh water throughout tropical regions. The flowers vary from blue to white or, as in the top photograph, combine both colours.

251

The Kimberley

The Kimberley

One of the short-necked turtles, *Emydura australis*, enters a stream.

Previous pages
Cabbage-tree palms (*Livistona* sp.) growing in the Bungle Bungles.

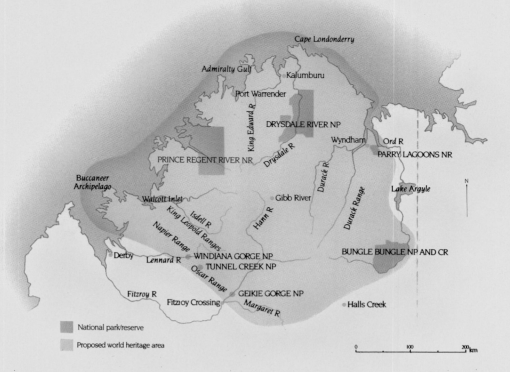

The Kimberley shares most of its species of flora and fauna with other areas of tropical Australia. Spinifex and other tussock grasses cover much of the more arid regions; mangroves grow extensively along stretches of its coast; stands of paperbark and red gums grow in gorges forged by streams through the limestone ranges; rock wallabies clamber over its rocky outcrops; freshwater crocodiles bask on its riverbanks and float, log-like, in its streams and waterholes; the dangerous saltwater crocodile inhabits its estuaries; a diversity of long-legged wading birds invade its swamps and lagoons, which are often covered with the broad leaves and large blooms of numerous species of waterlilies.

But some of the plant and animal life is distinctive. On the plains and in the limestone ranges grow the remarkable boab trees with their massive bulging trunks and antler-like branches. In summer these trees, which can live for more than a thousand years, produce large white flowers. In the several hundred patches of rainforest are over 250 endemic plant species, ranging from substantial trees to small shrubs. The mangrove swamps contain at least two mangrove species that are unknown elsewhere in Australia.

These mangrove colonies support an exceptionally rich birdlife, including one regional endemic, the rare and elusive brown-tailed flycatcher. So too do the heavily vegetated gorges, the extensive grasslands and the rainforest pockets. On the grasslands it is not unusual to see flocks of bustards, birds that seldom occur elsewhere in large numbers.

The karst landscapes and tussock grasslands in the Kimberley offer an ideal habitat for a range of smaller reptiles, including several lizards that are restricted to the region. One of these, a rock-dwelling velvet gecko, was recently discovered near Kalumburu in the extreme north. A rarely seen marsupial, the scaly-tailed possum, is also found only in rocky parts of the Kimberley; while the once widespread golden bandicoot, less restricted in its habitat, but also common among rocks, has become restricted to the north-western Kimberley and Barrow Island.

Blending almost perfectly with the colour of the rocks which are its favourite habitat is the spiny knob-tailed gecko (*Nephrurus asper*). Despite its fearsome appearance, enhanced by the spiny eruptions that cover its body and short stumpy tail, and despite the seeming hostility of its aggressive display, it is harmless to humans. Like other small reptiles of the arid areas, it lives mainly in spinifex and eats insects.

Previous pages

Boab trees (*Adansonia gregorii*), with their massive and often gnarled trunks, are among the region's most distinctive types of vegetation.

Disturbed while basking in the sun on a rocky ledge, this brown tree snake (*Boiga irregularis*) rears up in a characteristic looping movement to strike at an intruder. This snake inhabits a variety of habitats throughout the northern half of the continent, from tropical rainforests to dry woodlands. It also extends into New Guinea and Indonesia.

A green tree frog (*Litoria splendida*) moves towards water across rocks, using the sticky pads on the underside of the prominent digital discs to gain a firm footing. This photograph shows a number of features that characterise many *Litoria* species: the variegated green colour; the distinct and prominent tympanum, or ear covering; webbing between the toes; and the narrow horizontal slit shape of the pupil.

*T*his close-up photograph of the head of a little eagle (*Hieraaetus morphnoides*) shows clearly the erect crest feathers that distinguish this species. This voracious predator occurs throughout its range in a dark and a light phase, and here we see the chestnut colour that characterises birds of the light phase. The little eagle grows to about half the size of the wedge-tailed eagle.

The impression of serenity created by still water and the large floating leaves and purple-tinged blooms of waterlilies (*Nymphaea violacea*) can be rudely shattered by the sudden emergence of a lurking predator. In this case the predatory reptile is an olive python (*Liasis olivaceus*). This usually nocturnal snake is found, mainly in rocky locations, across the far north of Australia. It grows to about three and a half metres long and is non-venomous.

*T*urkey bush (*Calytrix exstipulata*)

*G*revillea pteridifolia

*B*oab (*Adansonia gregorii*)

*S*ticky kurrajong (*Sterculia viscidula*)

*G*iant milkweed (*Calotropis procera*)

*W*aterlily (*Nymphaea gigantea*)

*T*ribulopis bicolor

A selection of flowering plants seen in the Kimberley region. All but one of them are natives that bring colourful relief to a generally rugged and often monochrome landscape. The exception is the giant milkweed, an introduced and hardy noxious weed that is creating problems in the area. The large blooms of the boab are believed to be pollinated by bats. The deciduous sticky kurrajong is a common tree in the Kimberley.

Above and right
*F*reshwater crocodiles (*Crocodylus johnstoni*) are common in the many inland streams and lagoons of the Kimberley, in both muddy and clear water. They can be seen floating like partly submerged logs, with only their scaly backs and long, slender snouts visible, or basking on banks or rock ledges. Unlike the larger saltwater crocodiles, freshwater crocodiles pose no threat to humans.

Above
*A*n inhabitant of more arid areas, *Cyclorana australis* is distributed widely across northwestern Australia, extending south to the Alice Springs area. It is a large, broad-headed frog that can grow to ten centimetres long. Because of the width of its head it has a huge gaping mouth.

A yabby, or freshwater crayfish (*Cherax* sp.) in Tunnel Creek, the site of a famous limestone cave in the Napier Range. Of the three most commonly encountered genera of freshwater crayfish, *Cherax* is the only one that occurs in the more arid parts of Australia. Species of this genus are distinguishable by the absence of spines on their bodies.

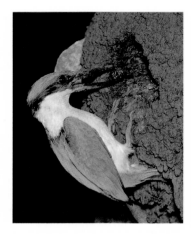

*I*n Australia the collared kingfisher (*Halcyon chloris*) is predominantly green and occurs only in mangroves around the coast of the northern half of the continent. It is widespread throughout much of southeast Asia where, in many places, it is much less specialised in its habitat and is more variously and brightly coloured.

*S*altwater crocodiles (*Crocodylus porosus*) occur commonly in the estuaries and inlets along the Kimberley coast and frequently lurk among stands of mangroves. These large and deadly predators typically swim or float partly submerged, with the top of the head and the nostrils above the water. When the crocodile submerges with its prey, valves close off the nostrils and make them watertight.

Right

*T*he tidal mudflats that characterise the estuaries of many of the Kimberley's rivers contain extensive mangrove stands. These support an abundance of plants and animals, including a wealth of birdlife.

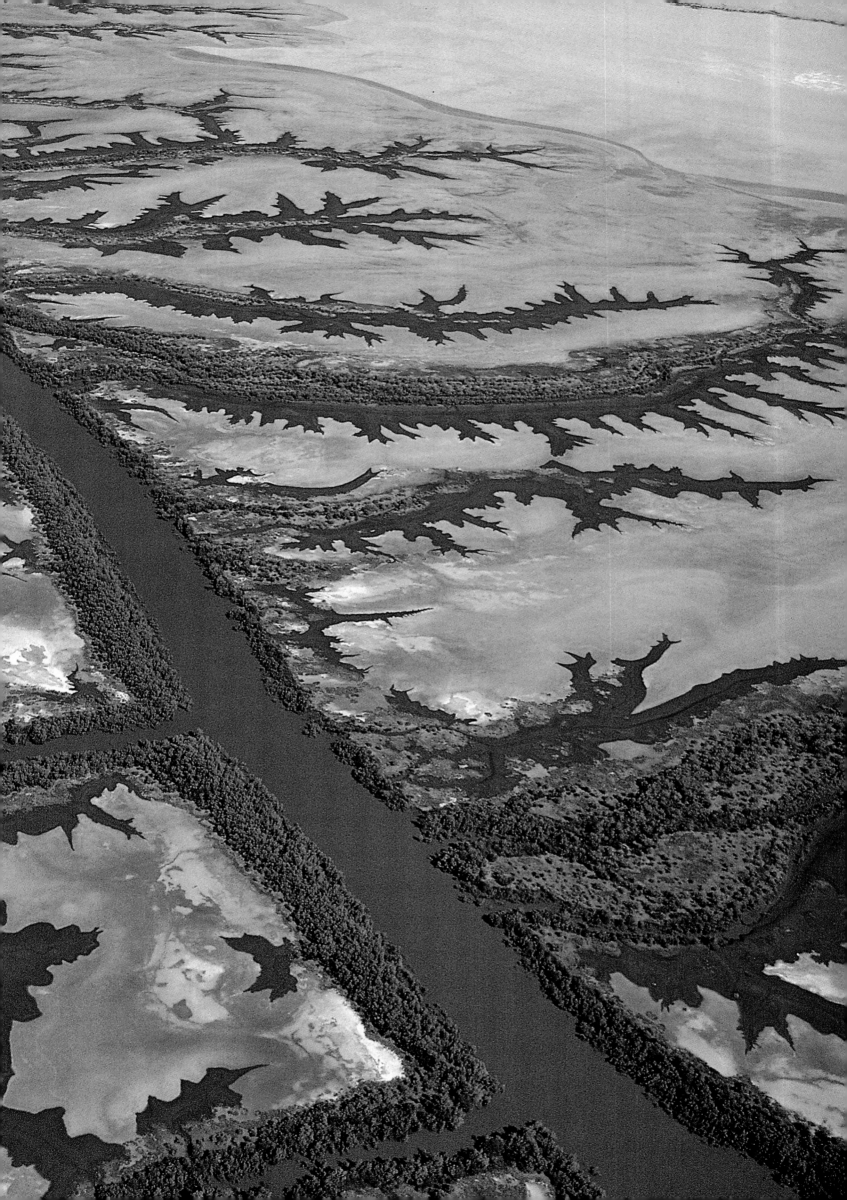

A true Kimberley endemic, the scaly-tailed possum (*Wyulda squamicaudata*) exists only, although sometimes abundantly, in various rocky locations in the region. Its name comes from the rough naked tail that winds around the trunks of trees during the possum's nocturnal foraging among the branches, mainly for blossoms and fruits. During the day it dwells among rocky boulders and is hardly ever seen. Little is known of its breeding habits. It grows to a total length of about seventy centimetres, just under half of which is accounted for by the tail.

Rock-rats are creatures of the arid centre and north, and of the three species, the common rock-rat (*Zyzomys argurus*) is the most widely distributed, extending across the north of the continent and occurring also in the Pilbara. It is remarkable particularly for the thickness of its long tail which, if it is intact, usually exceeds the animal's head and body length of about ten centimetres.

A pair of northern quolls (*Dasyurus hallucatus*) mating. These small marsupials mate in June and a litter of up to eight young is born the following month. The female has no pouch but the area around her nipples becomes surrounded by a flap of skin soon before mating. Northern quolls occur mainly in rocky habitats in open country across most of northern Australia. They are omnivores, consuming other, smaller mammals as well as insects and a variety of fruits.

*T*he northern brown bandicoot (*Isoodon macrourus*) inhabits a range of environments from savannah grasslands to thick forests. It is distributed widely along the east coast from north of Sydney and also occurs in Arnhem Land and the Kimberley.

The Kimberley is one of the few locations in which the bustard (*Ardeotis australis*) still occurs in large numbers. It was once common in grasslands throughout most of the continent. Though slow to take to the air, these large birds are strong fliers and can migrate long distances.

In his breeding plumage the male purple-crowned wren (*Malurus coronatus*) bears the bright purple crown patch that gives this bird its popular name. For the rest of the time, about half the year, the male has the general brown colouration of the female. These birds frequent moist forested areas in limited parts of the north and northwest.

*R*estricted to a small area in the northwest, the brown-tailed flycatcher (*Microeca tormenti*) inhabits mangrove swamps and forests.

*B*oth the male and female Gouldian finch (*Erythrura gouldiae*) are exquisitely coloured, with the female (*top*) displaying the more delicate pastel shades. They range across most of far northern Australia where there are lightly wooded grasslands and a ready supply of water.

A male star finch (*Neochmia ruficauda*), recognisable by its startlingly red beak and face, approaches its nest of grasses, built in a shrub. These seed-eaters frequent bushier grassland throughout northern Australia, always remaining close to water.

*A*lthough most Gouldian finches have black faces, red-faced members of the species are not uncommon. Less common, but sometimes encountered, are yellow-faced Gouldian finches. The species name of these birds was bestowed by the nineteenth-century naturalist and illustrator, John Gould.

The fixed, penetrating stare of a masked owl (*Tyto novaehollandiae*). Similar to the barn owl, the masked owl has a more limited distribution, being absent from the arid centre of the continent. It mainly inhabits wooded areas where it roosts during the day in the hollows of trees or even in the foliage but is found in treeless areas where there are caves. It is a nocturnal predator on native and introduced mammals, as well as on birds and reptiles.

The velvet gecko, *Oedura kalumburu*, an endemic of the Kimberley, has only recently been described and classified. A rock-dwelling species, it is named after the place in the extreme north of the Kimberley near which it most commonly occurs. Its smooth, slender and broadly striped body seems to accentuate its wide head and large round eyes, and the variegated colours of its body throw into relief the steely grey of its tail.

*R*estricted to the northern half of the continent, the ghost bat (*Macroderma gigas*) is found spasmodically in habitats as various as tropical rainforests and arid deserts. It is unique among Australian bats in that it is carnivorous, preying nocturnally on a range of vertebrates and invertebrates. It is the largest of the world's so-called 'microbats'.

*B*lack flying foxes (*Pteropus alecto*) are the largest of Australia's flying foxes. They roost, often in huge colonies, hanging head downward from the branches of trees, their dark wings drawn in like capes close to their bodies. They are abundant in mangrove areas and swamps around northern coastal areas and sometimes occur in moist forests. At night these winged mammals travel long distances to feed on figs and other fruits as well as tree blossoms.

*T*he ghost bat, when seen close up, is a bizarre-looking animal. Inordinately long ears, joined together well above the skull, and a prominent noseleaf contribute to the strangeness of its appearance. This bat is now considered endangered as very few large populations are known to exist and it seems sensitive to human intrusions into its varied habitats.

Top
*T*he long leaves and red fruit of the screw pine (*Pandanus darwinensis*), one of five *Pandanus* species that are common, along rivers and creeks and in swamps, in the Kimberley.

Above
A forest of *Livistona eastonii*, an endemic Kimberley palm.

Left
*C*abbage-tree palms (*Livistona* sp.) and other trees and bushes take precarious root in the meagre soil that has gathered in crevices in this Kimberley cliff face.

Right
A moist gully, sheltered by giant boulders, is able to support a diversity of vegetation including cabbage-tree palms, and species of *Eucalyptus*, *Acacia* and *Gardenia*, as well as low shrubs and grasses.

Shark Bay

Shark Bay

Shark Bay is the most southerly point at which the dugong occurs year round.

Previous pages
Extensive beds of seagrass are a feature of the
Shark Bay environment and an important dugong habitat.

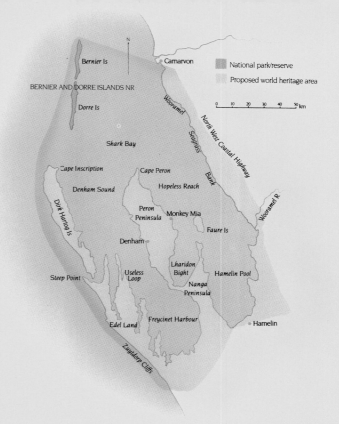

It is its marine flora and fauna that make Shark Bay uniquely significant. The turquoise and highly saline waters of this bay play host to a range of large marine animals, including dolphins, manta rays, whales and several species of sharks. Shark Bay also provides a habitat for a large population of dugongs, one of the world's rarer and endangered marine mammals, and is the most southerly point at which these animals occur throughout the year. Dugongs are the only herbivorous marine mammals and in Shark Bay they are sustained almost exclusively by the vast beds of seagrasses that are a feature of the bay, especially along its eastern side.

The numerous species of seagrasses support other animal species, including the large green and loggerhead turtles that are common at Shark Bay, by providing both a source of food and an important foraging environment. A wall of seagrass helps to maintain the high salinity of the waters of Hamelin Pool, in the southeast corner of the bay, where there exists the world's most abundant growth of algal stromatolites.

Shark Bay's land fauna is also of great significance. In particular, the spinifex-covered Bernier and Dorre islands provide refuge for numerous species of mammals that no longer exist, or are found only in isolated pockets, on the mainland. Among these are the banded and rufous hare-wallabies and the barred bandicoot. Even more specialised in its range is the tiny, but distinctive, Shark Bay mouse which is restricted to Bernier Island.

Seabirds, not surprisingly, feature prominently in this environment. The largest of them are the white-bellied sea-eagles and the ospreys which build their nests on headlands overlooking the bay.

Among the many reptiles adapted to the fairly arid conditions, the most conspicuous, because of its size and arresting looks, is the shingleback. Less obvious are a number of smaller endemic creatures, including a legless lizard and the recently discovered sandhill frog.

Shark Bay's vegetation consists mainly of grasses, especially spinifex, and low shrubs. As in many parts of Western Australia, a profusion of wildflowers enlivens the area in spring.

The extremely high salinity of the water of Hamelin Pool in Shark Bay has proved ideal for the growth of stromatolites. These ancient lifeforms occur in a variety of sometimes bizarre shapes. They are the product of the gradual accretion, over millions of years, of limestone sediments trapped by blue-green algae, or cyanophytes. They are among the oldest forms of life on earth.

Green turtles (*Chelonia mydas*) occur in considerable numbers at Shark Bay. Unlike other sea turtles, adult green turtles are not generally carnivorous but feed on algae and marine plants. Juveniles, however, are carnivores. These large turtles mate in the sea and the female lays her eggs on a beach in a depression in the sand. More than 100 eggs can be laid. The female covers the eggs with sand and returns to the water. The eggs hatch in just over two months and the young make their first precarious journey to the sea. While the adult turtles, which grow to about a metre long, are rarely preyed upon, the young are an easy target for seabirds. The bottom photograph shows a normal and a rare albino juvenile green turtle.

A thick-billed grasswren (*Amytornis textilis textilis*) on its partly domed nest of sticks and grass. These nests are usually built quite close to the ground in saltbushes. This relatively plain little bird lives on the scrubby plains of arid areas in the southern half of the continent. Shark Bay is at the northern limit of its range in Western Australia.

*I*n the arid environment around Shark Bay the decaying woody remains of shrubs are often found littering the desert sands. A number of prostrate shrubs, such as hardy and tough-leaved varieties of pigface, are well-suited to the prevailing conditions and many blossom colourfully. The one shown here is round-leaved pigface (*Disphyma crassifolium*).

Right

*E*xcept for a small area in central Australia, Bernier and Dorre islands provide the only remaining habitats for the rufous hare-wallaby (*Lagorchestes hirsutus*). It lives among spinifex vegetation, feeding on spinifex seeds and other plant matter.

Left

*T*he sandy landscape surrounding Shark Bay supports predominantly stunted vegetation, including various species of tussock grasses (*Triodia* and *Plectrachne* spp.). Wattles (*Acacia*) are the most commonly occurring shrubs.

Bernier and Dorre islands contain the only remaining populations of the banded hare-wallaby (*Lagostrophus fasciatus*), once distributed throughout southwest Western Australia but not recorded on the continent in more than eighty years. As the only surviving member of a kangaroo subfamily containing the extinct short-faced kangaroos, it is of immense biological importance.

Dunnarts belong to the family Dasyuridae, which also includes antechinuses, planigales, phascogales and quolls. Because of their appearance, and despite their predatory nature, these small carnivorous marsupials are often referred to as marsupial mice. Most dunnarts, like the recently discovered *Sminthopsis dolichura*, are predominantly insect eaters.

Its blunt nose and, more importantly, its black-flecked brown back and white sides and belly are the distinguishing features of the Shark Bay mouse (*Pseudomys praeconis*). This small rodent now seems to be restricted to Bernier Island where it inhabits sandy dunes among clumps of spinifex grass. It is thought to feed on flowers, as well as the stems and leaves of plants.

Another marsupial now found only on Bernier and Dorre islands, the barred bandicoot (*Perameles bougainville*) spends its days on sand dunes in a nest, lined with twigs and other plant matter, in a well-hidden burrow. At dusk it emerges to feed on small invertebrates, seeds and fruits.

Right
The sandhill frog (*Arenophryne rotunda*), a recently discovered species, endemic to Shark Bay.

*E*xtensive meadows of seagrass, which rely on sunlight for photosynthesis, thrive in the relatively shallow waters of Shark Bay. They support a range of marine animals, including seasnakes, turtles and the bay's large dugong population. The vast Wooramel seagrass bank, on the eastern side of the bay, covers an area of 117 000 hectares. In the estuary of the Wooramel River is a growth of tropical seagrass which is the main summer haunt of the dugongs.

Below

*T*he mouth and snout of a dugong (*Dugong dugon*). The large upper lip is used to manoeuvre seagrass, the dugong's staple food, into its mouth. The nostrils remain closed while the animal is submerged, opening to take in air when it surfaces.

*J*uvenile dugongs are carried around on their mothers' backs for up to two years. A single young is usually born about a year after mating and will not itself be capable of reproducing before it is about ten or more years old. This slow rate of reproduction has made the dugong vulnerable to extinction in areas where it is not protected.

284

A group of dugongs swimming in
the hypersaline waters of Hamelin
Pool. Dugongs are propelled mainly
by their broad horizontal tail flukes
which move slowly up and down as
the animal swims. The small
forelimbs help to keep the large body
stable and are used for changing
direction. The dugong's tail is
thought to have provided the
inspiration for mermaid legends.
Dugongs in Shark Bay migrate
seasonally to different areas of the
bay, seemingly in search of the
warmest water.

The handsome head of the white-bellied sea eagle (*Haliaeetus leucogaster*). This bird is distributed around most of the Australian coast and some inland areas. It is often seen flying over Shark Bay from its nesting sites on the headlands.

Below

A pair of ospreys (*Pandion haliaetus*) on their large nest of sticks high above the water. Ospreys are fishing hawks that breed most commonly on offshore islands. Often mistaken for sea eagles, they can be distinguished by the bowed shape of their wings while in flight, by the dark patch behind the eyes and by the ring of darker feathers around their neck.

Although more usually associated with the inland, Australia's largest bird of prey, the wedge-tailed eagle (*Aquila audax*) is frequently seen near Shark Bay. It is a carrion eater which, despite its reputation, seldom attacks healthy animals.

With its bulky pouch tucked away as it preens its feathers, this pelican (*Pelecanus conspicillatus*) appears sleeker than usual. In coastal areas like Shark Bay pelicans often congregate on small offshore islands which they share with terns, gulls and other seabird species. They nest on platforms of sticks and plant matter on beaches or sandbars.

Left

Shark Bay is almost at the northern limit of the Pacific gull's (*Larus pacificus*) range, which extends around the southern coasts to southern New South Wales. It is remarkable for its deep bulky bill which, in western birds, is banded at the tip with bright red. The upper part of the bills of eastern birds is uniformly orange-yellow. The Pacific gull is the largest of Australian gulls.

Manta rays (*Manta birostris*), more typically a tropical species, are nevertheless often encountered in the waters of Shark Bay. These huge marine animals can grow to widths of up to seven metres. They feed on small crustaceans and are completely harmless to humans and most marine animals. These rays frequently make spectacular leaps from the water, hitting the surface again with thunderous splashes.

The streamlined silver shapes of a school of barracuda (*Sphyraena*). These large ocean fish can grow to two metres long and are often feared by divers because of their size and their carnivorous ways. They are aggressive and will sometimes approach humans, often in order to investigate reflecting objects that divers are wearing.

Dolphins (*Tursiops truncatus*) are more numerous in Shark Bay than the other marine mammals. One group regularly visits the beach at Monkey Mia where the dolphins allow themselves to be hand-fed and stroked by humans. Such interaction is known nowhere else in the world.

An olive seasnake (*Aipysurus laevis*) swims over one of the rare coral patches that occur where bay waters meet the warmer waters of the Indian Ocean. Seasnakes in Shark Bay forage for fish among the prolific seagrass beds. Although they stay submerged for long periods, seasnakes must surface regularly in order to breathe. While underwater their nostrils are closed off by flaps of skin.

Below
Oyster shells with pearls. The town of Denham was established almost a century ago to support pearlers.

A male white-winged fairy wren (*Malurus leucopterus leucopterus*) brings food to its young. This wren, which is widely distributed over most of the inland, occurs in a black form only on Barrow and Dirk Hartog islands. Elsewhere the male is a bright cobalt blue. Throughout its entire range the adult female has pale brown plumage with a dull blue tail. These birds build covered nests of grasses in bushes or tall grass tussocks.

The legless lizard (*Aprasia haroldi*), which is endemic to Shark Bay, is one of only nine species of this genus of worm lizards found in Australia. These small sand burrowers grow to about fifteen centimetres long. They are not entirely legless, as they have minute vestigial hind limbs.

Left
*T*he shingleback (*Trachydosaurus rugosus*) is the most conspicuous of the many skinks in the Shark Bay region. It grows to more than forty centimetres long and is an omnivore, feeding on flowers, fruits, snails and carrion. It occurs widely in arid areas of southern Australia.

Above
A range of stunted shrub vegetation, including species of *Acacia*, at Monkey Mia on the eastern side of the Peron Peninsula.

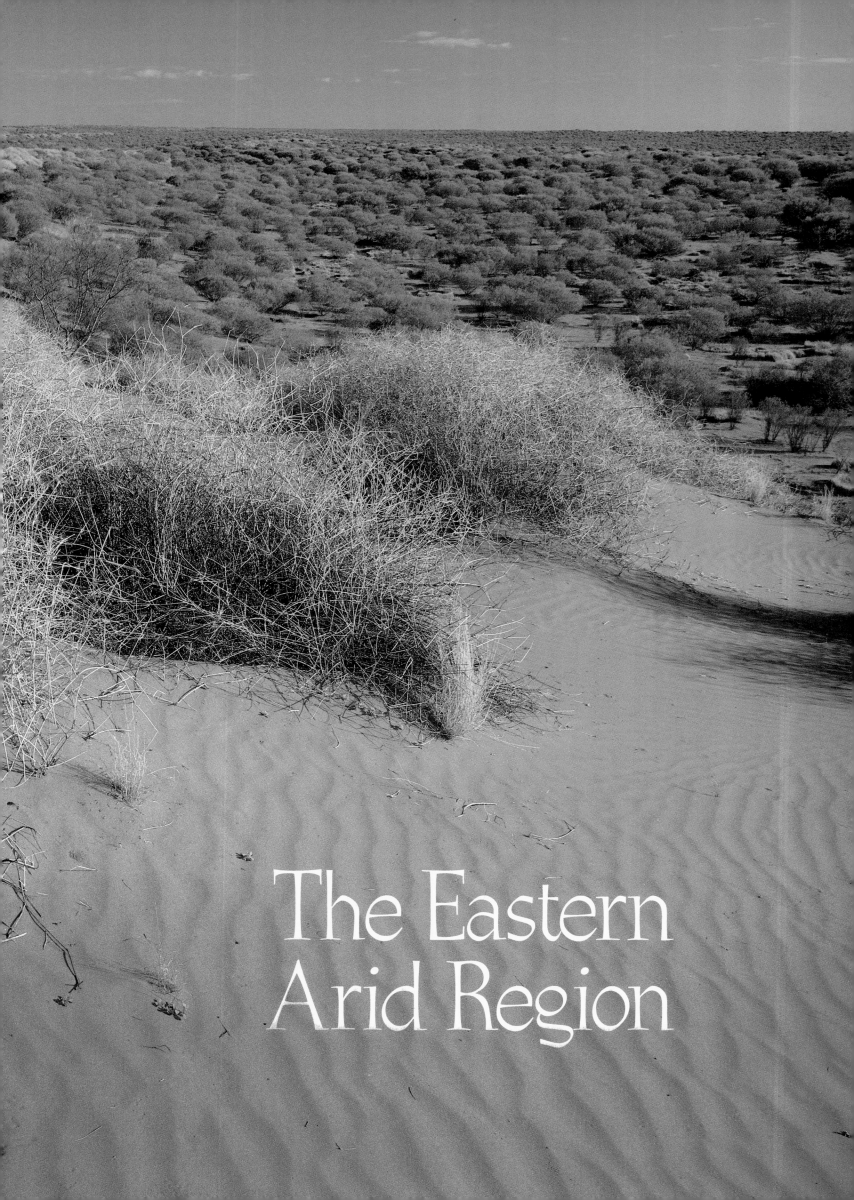

The Eastern
Arid Region

The Eastern Arid Region

A water-holding frog (*Cyclorana platycephalus*) in the mud of a dried-out waterhole.

Previous pages
*G*rey clumps of sandhill cane-grass (*Zygochloa paradoxa*) and dark green
shrubs of dune wattle (*Acacia ligulata*) grow in the Simpson Desert.

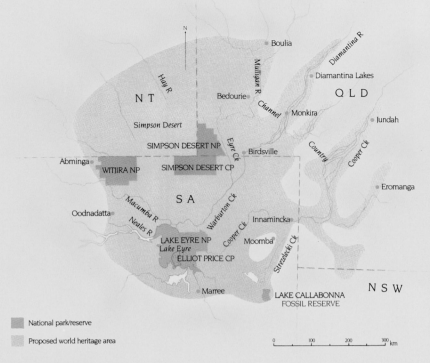

National park/reserve

Proposed world heritage area

0   100   200   300 km

Within the areas which collectively make up the eastern arid region lie the driest and least fertile parts of the continent. Large expanses of it, particularly the desolate gibber plains of Sturt's Stony Desert, support at most only the sparsest of plant growth, and sometimes none at all. The vast Simpson Desert, which occupies about half the region, is typified by long wind-created sand dunes, bare on top but stabilised on the sides and in the depressions by numerous grasses and small shrubs. Dense clumps of cane-grass, along with species of spinifex, are particularly common here, as are saltbushes, peas and a variety of wattles, including the widely occurring sandhill wattle. At the edges of the Simpson Desert occur rare stands of waddy wood, a tall pine-like wattle that dominates surrounding plants.

It is mainly in the few places where there is permanent water and along the beds of creeks that flow as a result of spasmodic or seasonal rains that more substantial shrubs and trees occur. The dry beds of streams are often marked by stands of coolibah, river red gum, gidgee and mulga.

Many of the animals that frequent the region show a high degree of adaptation to the arid conditions. Some, like the kowari, the plains rat and the fawn hopping mouse — all endemic to the eastern arid region — are able to obtain all their moisture needs from the food they eat. They avoid extremes of heat by spending their days in deep subterranean burrows. The water-holding frog stays underground during droughts, emerging to breed and replenish its water supply when the rains come. The endangered bilby, which has fairly recently become restricted to the more arid areas, shows a less complete adaptation. Although it can exist without surface water and shelters in burrows from the daytime heat, it is susceptible to heat stress. Its rate of reproduction may be slower in the more arid environments.

Birds of prey, grass finches and flocks of parrots are frequently seen in these and other arid zones. Almost never encountered is the night parrot, a nocturnal bird that nests under spinifex clumps and one of the world's rarest and least known birds. An endangered and very localised endemic is the Eyrean grasswren which lives among cane-grass clumps.

*B*earded dragons (*Amphibolurus barbatus*) are found in habitats as diverse as wet forests and the arid sun-cracked desert shown here. In different environments this species varies its colour to blend with its surroundings. Individuals can also change their colour. When threatened this spiny lizard stages an impressive show of aggression, opening its mouth wide to reveal the bright yellow interior, hissing loudly, inflating its body with air and extending the spines below its throat to display its 'beard'.

*E*ndemic to the eastern arid region, the extremely venomous fierce snake (*Parademansia microlepidota*) is rarely seen. It grows to a little more than two metres long and is often mistaken for the more common taipan which, however, inhabits more northerly and westerly arid regions. It feeds during the day on small mammals, birds and reptiles and can move very swiftly in pursuit of its prey.

Adapted, like the bearded dragon, to widely differing habitats and ranging over most of the continent, the much smaller Bynoe's gecko (*Heteronotia binoei*) also varies in colour to match its environment. Black and white tubercles cover this gecko's back and tail to produce a mottled effect which is enhanced by the presence of small granules. On each of its forelimbs, between the digits, there is a conspicuous claw. Bynoe's gecko grows to about ten centimetres long and is a ground dweller.

Scorpions (order Scorpiones) were among the first animals to emerge from the sea and adapt to life on dry land, and are related to primitive forms of spiders. They differ from the spiders of today in that they lack silk glands and spinnerets, and males have no sperm-storing bulbs in their palps. Scorpions use their large palps to hold their prey — which can be insects, spiders and even other scorpions — while they devour it. A venomous sting is contained in the long tapering tail that arches over the scorpion's back.

*O*range chats (*Ephthianura aurifrons*) range over most of the drier parts of southern Australia but display a particular liking for the vicinity of salt lakes. They build cupshape nests close to the ground in samphire or saltbushes, or in grass clumps. They move around in flocks, but will sometimes settle for long periods in particular areas. The adult shown here feeding its chicks is a male. The female is paler in colour and lacks an orange tinge on the forehead. These tiny birds feed on the ground on insects, and possibly on nectar.

*L*ittle corellas (*Cacatua sanguinea*), like many other parrots, often flock in huge numbers, flying through the outback and renting the air with their harsh, raucous cries. These small white parrots move around the arid interior seeking out places where the seeds of native grasses are plentiful.

Far right

With its wing raised, this letter-winged kite (*Elanus scriptus*) displays its distinctive bold black wing markings. A bird of the arid interior, it is a specialised predator on rodents, especially the long-haired rat.

Right

The little corella (*Cacatua sanguinea*) is widespread throughout the drier parts of the continent and occurs also in southern New Guinea. It nests in the hollows of trees. Pair-bonding is common and birds have been known to return repeatedly to the same nest.

Part of the floodplain caused by the periodic flooding of the Diamantina River after heavy summer rains. In years when rivers are swelled by northerly cyclonic rains substantial quantities of water can reach the normally dry bed of Lake Eyre, attracting forms of wildlife unusual in the dry interior to its shores. The dead tree dominating this scene is a river red gum.

As the floods subside some of the casualties caused by the inundation become obvious. In this expanse of mud, in the Simpson Desert, are the shells of myriad land snails drowned by the incursion of water.

As the waters spread through the channel country they move in well-worn channels in which vegetation is characteristically more developed than on the higher ground that the water does not reach. This is one of the many arms that branch out from the flooded Cooper's Creek.

The water-holding frog (*Cyclorana platycephalus*) takes advantage of the floodwaters to emerge from its burrow beneath the desert sand to breed, laying its eggs on the bottom of shallow pools. At these times it is very much in evidence. When the water subsides this large, rotund frog uses its hind limbs to burrow into the sand. It remains hidden in its burrow until the next rains come. It survives long dry spells using water in its bladder and in subcutaneous glands.

A Gould's goanna (*Varanus gouldii*) splashes through the shallow surface water. Although common in arid and semiarid areas, this large goanna is also at home in the moist forests where, instead of burrowing in sand, it will take up residence in the hollows of logs. In the desert it tends to be much lighter-coloured.

A stand of minni-ritchi (*Acacia cyperophylla*) grows in this dry watercourse in the Simpson Desert. This species is restricted to the Simpson Desert and the Queensland channel country. These small trees stand out strongly against the sparse surrounding vegetation.

Far right
*V*egetation and an accumulation of sand mark the course of this dried-up stream through the gibber desert.

*I*ts capacity to obtain all the fluid it needs from the grasses and insects it eats helps the fawn hopping mouse (*Notomys cervinus*) to survive on the arid plains that are its almost exclusive domain. During the day family groups of these small rodents remain well below the ground in burrows they have dug.

Downy swainsona
Swainsona swainsonioides

Dead finish
Acacia tetragonophylla

Two flowering plants of the desert: downy swainsona is a pea that grows in large clumps in heavier soils; dead finish will grow in much less favourable soils and can reach a height of five metres.

The Darling lily (*Crinum flaccidum*) is an adaptable plant, occurring widely throughout the continent and extending into arid regions.

Far right

Acacias are the tallest plants in this stretch of the extreme northeastern Simpson Desert.

Whereas in the Kimberley the bustard (*Ardeotis australis*) still roams the plains in large flocks, in the eastern arid region it is now only seen, and then rarely, singly or in pairs. The incidence of this bird has declined sharply with the spread of human settlement and as a result of the introduction of foxes.

Reddish brown like its habitat, the Eyrean grasswren (*Amytornis goyderi*) was long thought to be extinct until in 1961 a colony was discovered north of Lake Eyre. It lives among cane-grass sandhills in localised sections of the Simpson Desert.

Distinguishable by the thick black brush at the end of its tail, the kowari (*Dasyuroides byrnei*) is endemic to the eastern arid region. It is found mainly in gibber deserts and is a nocturnal predator on insects and small mammals.

*A*n adult male narrow-nosed planigale (*Planigale tenuirostris*) characteristically grasps its prey as it devours it. This tiny inhabitant of the eastern arid interior grows to a total length, including its tail, of little more than ten centimetres.

Right
*T*hick silver-grey fur characterises the plains rat (*Pseudomys australis*), a desert-dwelling rodent that can survive without access to water.

Landscapes covered with spinifex and tussock grasses are the kinds of environment in which the now endangered greater bilby (*Macrotis lagotis*) frequently occurs. These appealing animals, with their seemingly oversized ears and black and white tails, were once widespread over the central and southern parts of the continent, and extended well into the southeast. Now they occur only in isolated pockets throughout the arid zones where they have adapted less successfully than some other inhabitants. They have a low tolerance, for example, of extreme heat. They live in subterranean burrows during the day and it is thought that competition from rabbits for burrows has been a factor contributing to their decline. At night greater bilbies hunt energetically for insects. They probably also eat seed and fruits. A litter of up to three young is produced, and juveniles are able to leave the pouch after about three months.

Like some of the small native mammals whose habitats it threatens, the introduced camel (*Camelus dromedarius*) is well adapted to arid conditions. It retains fluid in its body tissues and can survive for extended periods without water or food. Thousands of feral camels roam the interior, often in mobs of several hundred.

Small mammals are the favourite prey of the ubiquitous dingo (*Canis familiaris dingo*). Infrequently seen in the driest regions during rainless summer periods, it is much more common during the cooler months when the moisture it obtains from its prey can allow it to go without drinking for days at a time.

Like camels, donkeys (*Equus asinus*) became superfluous as beasts of burden with the advent of motorised transport and were released in large numbers into the wild. They now wander over most of the arid interior, a major pest to pastoralists and a competitor with native animals for often scarce water and plants. Again like camels, they trample and destroy the burrows of small native mammals.

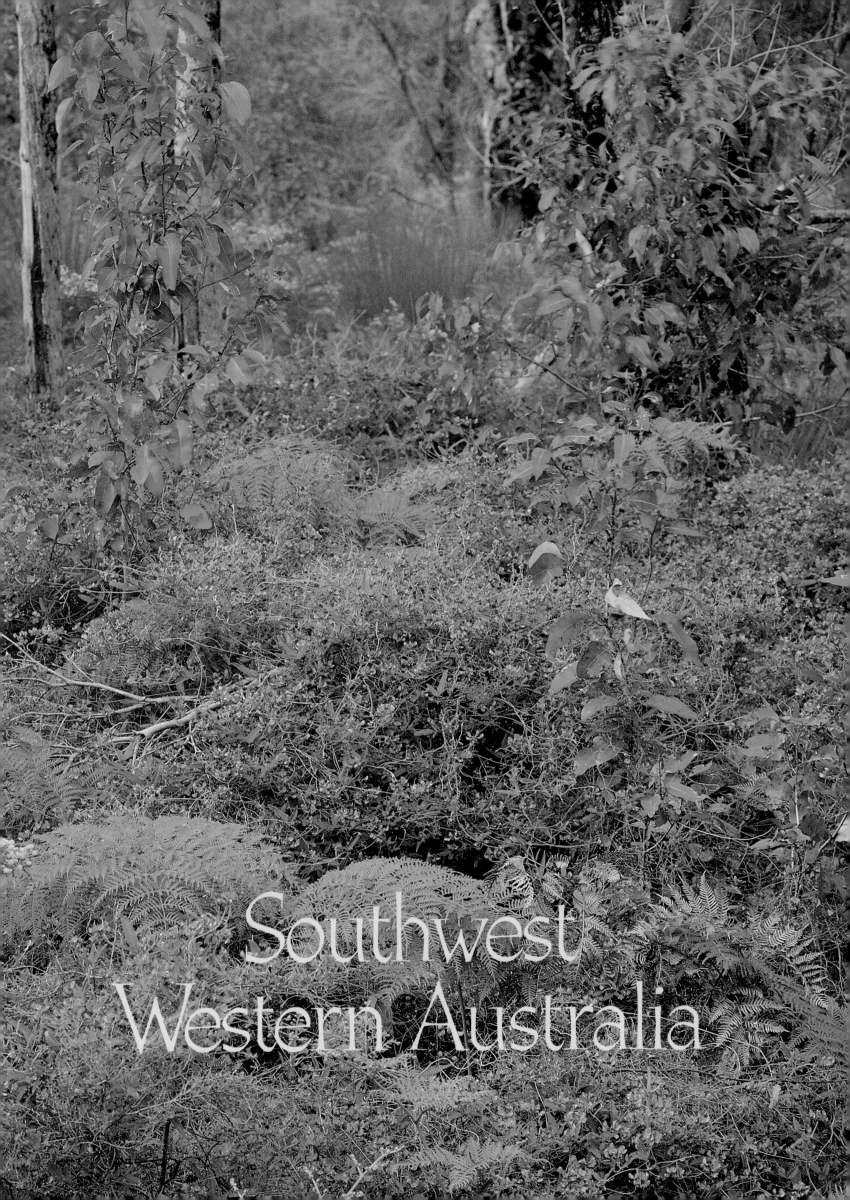

Southwest
Western Australia

Southwest Western Australia

*T*he numbat (*Myrmecobius fasciatus*) is a specialised feeder upon termites.

Previous pages
*I*n the understorey of this jarrah forest are the yellow blooms of wattles
(*Acacia* sp.) and the orange- red flowers of the coral vine (*Kennedia coccinea*).

The very southwest corner of the continent, an area generally noted for low summer rainfall and sandy or gravelly soils, is, perhaps surprisingly, the repository of some of the country's finest forests, containing species of trees that grow nowhere else. Towering forests of karri, majestic giants that soar to more than seventy metres, grow in sandy loam soils in a relatively high-rainfall area of the extreme southwest between Albany and Busselton. Less lofty, but just as remarkable in view of the nutrient-deficient soils in which they often grow, are the stands of jarrah, which grow in a wide area of the southwest from Perth south to Albany. Both karri and jarrah have suffered as a result of human intervention. Stands of karri were greatly depleted as land was cleared for farming; and jarrah, being a superb hardwood, has been extensively exploited for commercial purposes. Other eucalypts endemic to this region include the marri, a large bloodwood often found in association with jarrah, the tuart, and the huge red tingle.

In spring the understorey of many of these forests bursts into new life with the blossoming of wildflowers. Species of *Grevillea*, *Hakea*, *Acacia*, as well as orchids and peas, are among the most abundant of these native flowers, many of which are endemic to the region. But it is probably on the sandy plains to the north of Perth that wildflowers create the greatest spectacle, carpeting a normally monotonous, scrubby landscape with great expanses of vibrant colour. Among the plants that are familiar throughout the southwest, and endemic to it, are the ten species of *Agonis* — the white-flowering peppermint plants that range from low spreading shrubs to tall trees. The most eye-catching of the wattles, the prickly Moses, flowers profusely in winter.

The southwest supports a number of mammals that are endemic to the region. Perhaps the most familiar is the quokka, a small wallaby that abounds among the low scrub on Rottnest Island but which finds a more congenial environment in the moist forests further south. Another, rarely encountered and now considered endangered, is the numbat, a small termite-eating pouchless marsupial that lives largely in jarrah forests.

*K*arri (*Eucalyptus diversicolor*) is among the world's tallest trees, growing to between forty-five and seventy metres and, in rare cases, reaching ninety metres tall. It grows only in the southwest of Western Australia and thrives in high rainfall areas with deep loam soils. In some forests, such as the one shown at right northwest of Walpole, karri is the only dominant tree; in others, as in the photograph above, it occurs in association with other eucalypt species. The karri's smooth white trunk has a yellow, blue or pink tinge according to the season. Its species name derives from its large, lance-shaped leaves which are dark green above and pale green below.

Right
*K*arri forests are characterised by a dense layer of shrubs. In this forest, in the Warren National Park, the palm-like fronds in the left foreground belong to the cycad *Macrozamia riedlei*. The purple blooms are those of the native wisteria (*Hardenbergia comptoniana*) and the white flowers are *Clematis*. The taller shrub at right is the native willow (*Oxylobium lanceolatum*).

Southwest Western Australia is unsurpassed for the variety of its native flowers. In spring carpets of wildflowers produce dazzling kaleidoscopes of colour throughout many parts of the region, and nowhere more startlingly than on the sandplains north of Perth, dominated for most of the year by drab scrub vegetation. These and the following pages present a selection of the flowers in the southwest. The photograph above shows an expanse of paper daisies (*Helipterum roseum*).

Right

The honey possum (*Tarsipes rostratus*), a minute endemic of the southwest, probes flowers of nectar-producing plants with its long snout, extracting the pollen and nectar with its brush-like tongue. This animal is about to feed on a fox banksia (*Banksia sphaerocarpa*), a plant endemic to the region.

*B*lue lace flower
Trachymene coerulea

*K*angaroo paw
Anigozanthos sp.

*R*ed and green kangaroo paw
Anigozanthos manglesii

*W*oolly feather flower
Verticordia monadelpha

*S*carlet banksia
Banksia coccinea

*P*ink enamel orchid
Elythranthera emarginata

*C*law feather flower
Verticordia grandiflora

*S*tarflowers
Calytrix sp.

*D*ancing orchid
Caladenia discoidea

*P*imelea ferruginea

*R*ed lechenaultia
Lechenaultia formosa

*S*tarflowers
Calytrix sp.

Mountain bell
Darwinia collina

Royal hakea
Hakea victoria

Cranbrook bell
Darwinia meeboldii

Barrens regelia
Regelia velutina

Pink fairy
Caladenia latifolia

Blushing mountain bell
Darwinia leiostyla

Summer coppercups
Pileanthus filifolius

Lemon orchid
Thelymitra antennifera

Snakebush
Hemiandra pungens

Queen of Sheba orchid
Thelymitra variegata

*I*n many parts of the southwest, especially on poor soils containing a high proportion of lateritic limestone gravel and sand, jarrah (*Eucalyptus marginata*) grows in pure stands. In more alluvial soils it often occurs, as in both these photographs, with marri (*E. calophylla*). The jarrah trees can be distinguished by their reddish bark which peels off in strips. The marris have a smoother appearance and their trunks are greyish brown. When burnt, marris, which contain numerous gum veins, give out dark red kino. Jarrah, which is much less susceptible to 'veining', has been greatly exploited for the quality and durability of its timber. Both jarrah and marri grow to more than thirty metres tall; in some situations jarrah can reach to forty-five metres.

In the foreground of this sweeping view over the Stirling Ranges is a grass tree (*Xanthorrhoea* sp.), with erect spiky leaves. The shrubs with dark green leaves and tiny white blooms are peppermints (*Agonis* sp.), and the shrub with golden brown new leaves is a *Hakea*. The Stirling Ranges have a rich and diverse flora, with fifty recorded endemic species.

Right

The leaves of grass trees often prove congenial nesting places for the western pygmy possum (*Cercartetus concinnus*). Here the tiny animal sleeps during the day. It ventures out at night to feed in trees and bushes on nectar and insects.

The narrow black band of spines that runs down the back and tail of the western spiny-tailed gecko (*Diplodactylus spinigerus*) contrasts with the grey smoothness of the rest of its body. In common with several other members of its genus, this gecko is able to exude a thick, pungent fluid from its pores, probably as a means of defence.

Both *Crinea georgiana* (*below*) and *Litoria moorei* (*left and below left*) are endemic to the southwest. *L. moorei* is unusual among western frogs in that it breeds in summer. *C. georgiana* is restricted to the Darling Range and south coast.

The black tiger snake (*Notechis ater*),
photographed in the Stirling Range,
is one of Australia's most dangerous
snakes, possessing venom that affects
the nervous system, and can cause
death by asphyxiation. Normally
unaggressive, it reacts very strongly
to provocation, hissing loudly and
menacingly while keeping its head
and neck close to the ground. It
grows to about one and a half metres
long. Often found near water, this
snake is mainly diurnal and eats fish
as well as lizards, birds and mammals.

Significantly larger than its relative, the northern quoll, the western quoll (*Dasyurus geoffroii*) now occurs only in southwest Western Australia and Papua New Guinea. It was once widespread over much of the continent. It also differs from the omnivorous northern quoll in being more carnivorous, eating any vulnerable animals, dead or alive, that it encounters.

Right

Western grey kangaroos (*Macropus fuliginosus*) are the only large macropods to occur in the southwest of Western Australia. There is evidence to suggest that the species originated in this region. It is similar in appearance and habits to the eastern grey, with which it shares the eastern extremity of its range. It differs, but only subtly, in its more 'chocolate' tones, in the quality of its leather and in the odour of the males.

The red-tailed phascogale (*Phascogale calura*), once found in isolated pockets throughout the south and centre of the continent, is now restricted to drier woodlands in parts of southwest Western Australia. It feeds on small birds and mammals.

Yellow-footed antechinuses, or mardos (*Antechinus flavipes*), are common in eastern Australia, but in the west they occur only in the southwest corner. They have adapted to widely differing environments and are omnivorous, feeding mainly on insects, but also eating flowers, nectar and small vertebrates.

In southwest Western Australia Port Lincoln ringnecks (*Barnardius zonarius*) are popularly referred to as 'twenty-eight' parrots because of the three-syllabled call, fancifully thought to resemble the sound of the number, that is peculiar to members of the species in that region.

Western rosellas (*Platycercus icterosis*) are endemic to southwest Western Australia. They are common in timbered areas where they establish nests in the hollows of eucalypt trees. The bird shown here is a male. The female has a green head and chest and is generally less brightly coloured.

The splendid wren (*Malurus splendens*) is well named. The luminous blues and black of the male in his breeding plumage make this the most eye-catching of Australian wrens. However, its natural shyness and predilection for habitats where there is dense undergrowth mean that it seldom presents itself for human scrutiny.

Restricted to the southwestern corner of the continent, the western spinebill (*Acanthorhynchus superciliosus*) inhabits open woodland and heaths. It uses its curved bill to delve deep into flowers and extract their nectar. It is particularly partial to banksias.

*P*opularly associated with Western Australia, black swans (*Cygnus atratus*) are widespread throughout the southern half of the continent and extend north into eastern and central Queensland. Although they are graceful in the air, especially when flocks fly in V-formation, they are flightless during most of the summer while they are moulting. Black swans build their nests in reeds or on small islands. About six eggs are laid and these are incubated by both sexes for about six weeks.

*B*ecause they can breed at any time of the year, mature black swans are often seen in the company of several fluffy grey cygnets. By the time they are able to fly, at the age of four to five months, the young swans have acquired some brown plumage, and at the end of a year they have become black like the adults. They are sexually mature at eighteen months.

Left

A stand of red tingle (*Eucalyptus jacksonii*) in the Walpole–Nornalup National Park on the south coast. These large trees, which often occur in association with karri, can grow to more than sixty metres high and achieve a trunk diameter of more than four metres. Exceptional examples of much larger trees have also been recorded. They grow in deep loam soils in an area of the south coast near Walpole where there is a high annual rainfall. Their bark has a distinct reddish tinge and the trees are crowned with dense foliage.

*B*est known as an inhabitant of the relatively barren Rottnest Island, the quokka (*Setonix brachyurus*) is also common in the much more moist and well-vegetated extreme southwest. Although this small wallaby, endemic to the southwest, can survive for long periods without water, summer conditions on Rottnest often prove too harsh, and result in the death of many animals.

*P*art of the superb Ludlow State Forest, a tuart forest north of Busselton. Around Busselton is the southernmost area in which tuart (*Eucalyptus gomphocephala*) occurs. These large, grey-barked trees can grow as tall as forty metres. They are restricted to the coastal plain south of the Hill River on sandy loams which overlie limestone.

Along Western Australia's rocky coastline salt-tolerant plants survive in rock crevices despite regular exposure to salt spray. The prostrate plants growing here, in part of the William Bay National Park, include species of *Carpobratus* and *Tetragonia*. The erect grey shrubs are *Olearia axillaris*.

Australian sea-lions (*Neophoca cinerea*) inhabit rocky shores and sandy beaches on islands off the coast of southwest Western Australia. They are the only eared seals that are endemic to Australia.

Right
A green alga grows in the sand among sea-battered rocks on the south coast.

Right
Seaweeds and marine animals, washed ashore by heavy seas, bring an attractive, though temporary, splash of colour to a south coast beach.

The Alps

The Alps

*E*astern grey kangaroos (*Macropus giganteus*) have adapted to subalpine conditions.

Previous pages

*M*ountain gum, narrow-leaved peppermint and alpine ash are
prominent eucalypt species throughout the Australian Alps.

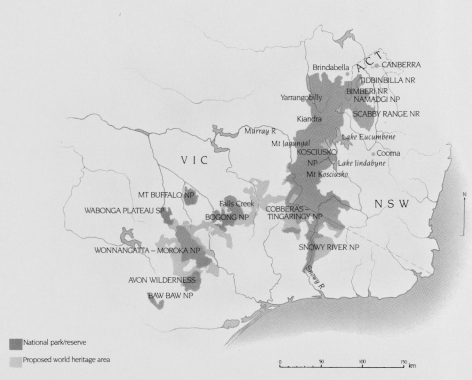

National park/reserve
Proposed world heritage area

Sclerophyll forests occupy much of the slopes and subalpine regions of the Australian Alps, which contain a more abundant and varied concentration of eucalypts than any other area of Australia. Most characteristic of the area is the very distinctive snow gum, with its often distorted forms, variegated trunks and variety of shapes and sizes. It grows, usually as a mallee or severely bent tree, at altitudes of almost 2000 metres — higher than any other Australian tree — and is the only tree to occur beyond an altitude of about 1500 metres. Further down, other eucalypts — notably alpine ash from about 600 metres and mountain gum from about 900 metres — overtop other trees and on the lower slopes the forests contain a wide range of eucalypt species, including tall stands of stringybarks and candlebarks.

Above the treeline heath and grasslands predominate. These are characterised by low and prostrate shrubs and species of snow grass. One of these shrubs, the mountain plum-pine, is the Australian Alps' only native conifer. The summer landscape on these higher slopes glows with colour as a host of wildflower species — peas, daisies, billy buttons, buttercups, grevilleas and many other others — burst into bloom. Patches of sphagnum bog create areas of deep green which contrast with the greenish grey of the grasses and the varied hues of the wildflowers.

It is these sphagnum bogs that provide a habitat for one of the region's endemic animals. The unmistakable and flamboyantly marked corroboree frog burrows deep down in the bogs, remaining under the snow during the winter. Another regional endemic, restricted to limited areas near Mt Hotham and Mt Kosciusko, is the tiny mountain pygmy possum, discovered only in 1966, and before that thought to have been long extinct. Lower down, the limestone country near the Snowy River is the only remaining habitat in Victoria for the brush-tailed rock wallaby, a species very sensitive to the effects of interference with its environment.

A bird closely associated with the Australian Alps is the gang-gang cockatoo, which breeds in the subalpine eucalypt forests during the summer and then disperses more widely with the onset of winter.

*P*erched picturesquely atop a narrow stalk this male flame robin (*Petroica phoenicea*) is on the alert for any movement that may betray the presence of an insect. Often confused with the scarlet robin, the flame robin has a smaller range than its close relative and is confined largely to Tasmania and the southeast of the continent where it frequents both the mountain forests and plains. The female is brown-breasted and lacks the fiery orange of the male.

*O*ne of the most distinctive and common birds in eastern Australia the pied currawong (*Strepera graculina*), with its jet black curved beak and plumage tinged with white, presents a sinister appearance that is accentuated by its yellow eyes and the haunting cry from which its name is derived. Often encountered in the built-up areas, pied currawongs usually breed in thick mountain forests. These sleek omnivores prey on insects, plants, carrion and even raid the nests of smaller birds to devour their chicks.

Right

*T*he gang-gang cockatoo (*Callocephalon fimbriatum*) was singled out by the nineteenth century naturalist and bird illustrator, John Gould, as the most interesting of Australian cockatoos. Despite the impression of ferocity imparted by its dishevelled comb it is one of the most approachable of birds. Similar in size and colouration to the galah, the gang-gang cockatoo is rarely seen outside a very limited area in the southeast of the continent, where it breeds in the alpine regions during the summer. It feeds noisily on seeds of native shrubs and trees such as eucalypts and, as here, acacias.

*T*he aptly named alpine celery (*Aciphylla glacialis*) has thick stems, prickly dissected leaves at ground level and distinctive clusters of tiny white scented flowers. Able to withstand extremes of cold, it grows in alpine regions, mainly above 1800 metres. Extensive grazing in the period up to the Second World War almost eliminated it in the Kosciusko National Park but conservation and protection measures since then have encouraged its regeneration. In the Victorian Alps continued grazing has rendered it quite rare in most areas.

*A*lpine hovea (*Hovea purpurea* var. *montana*), seen here in the foreground, flowers early in the high country, covering many an alpine slope with patches of purple and mauve, which stand out against the prevailing grey-greens of the snow grasses (*Poa* spp.). In the background are snow gums, and the shrubs in front of them are *Bossiaea folioso*.

*T*hese yellow billy buttons (*Craspedia* sp.), standing about forty centimetres from the ground on their long stems, were photographed at Mt Hotham in Victoria. Large numbers of these blooms are a feature of the alpine landscape in summer. While the yellow-flowered variety is the most familiar, billy buttons can range in colour from almost white to orange.

339

Although its tail which, at about fourteen centimetres is almost one and a half times as long as its body, is adapted to wrapping around branches, the mountain pygmy possum (*Burramys parvus*) lives and feeds on the ground rather than in trees. It is much rarer than other pygmy possums and is restricted to two small areas high in the Australian Alps. It is one of only two mammals that live the year round on the summit of Mt Kosciusko.

The brush-tailed rock wallaby (*Petrogale penicillata*) is still to be found in much of its range in eastern and central New South Wales, but its populations in Victoria are greatly reduced. In the Victorian Alps its survival is only reasonably secure in the area around the Snowy River gorge. This appealing marsupial, distinguished by its long, well-furred tail, light stripe on each cheek and the black stripe that runs from between the eyes to the back of the head, inhabits open eucalypt forests and grows to about half a metre long.

Right

Although it is one of the larger Australian possums, the small face of the greater glider (*Petauroides volans*) looks curiously out of proportion with its heavily furred body and long, bushy, straight tail. In flight, however, it is the essence of grace and aerobatic dexterity, being able to glide as far as a hundred metres and to execute sudden and radical changes of direction. Its sharp claws enable it to land vertically on the sides of eucalypts whose leaves form its sole source of food.

The progressive damming and siltation of the rivers of the Murray–Darling system over the last forty years or so have destroyed many of the deep rock pools in which the Macquarie perch (*Macquaria australasica*) lived and spawned. Its numbers have been greatly reduced and it is now considered an endangered species. It still finds a congenial habitat, however, in the cool waters of the Cotter River.

The attractively patterned alpine water skink (*Sphenomorphus kosciuskoi*) inhabits the heaths and woodlands of the Kosciusko area, but is also found in other high-altitude regions of New South Wales. Its distribution reaches as far north as the New England Tableland.

Right

Probably the most spectacular of Australia's frogs, the tiny corroboree frog (*Pseudophryne corroboree*) is endemic to the Australian Alps. The corroboree frog is named because its yellow and black colouration resembles Aboriginal ritual markings. It is unusual in that it moves by crawling rather than hopping. Growing to less than three centimetres long, it lives and breeds mainly in sphagnum moss bogs.

Also found in the waters of the Cotter River, the sleek and slender river blackfish (*Gadopsis mamoratus*) is more numerous and widespread throughout southeast Australia than the Macquarie perch, although its numbers, too, seem to be diminishing. It can in rare cases grow to a length of sixty centimetres, about twice the maximum length of the Macquarie perch. It prefers habitats where, as in this photograph, it can take shelter behind large rocks.

*S*preading fronds of the soft tree fern (*Dicksonia antarctica*) contribute to the lushness of this Snowy Mountains scene. These ferns are abundant in moist gullies in alpine regions. They can grow as tall as fifteen metres and sometimes exist in pure stands. The pith in the trunk is rich in starch and was removed and eaten by Aborigines. The large shrubs in the bottom of the gully are musk daisy-bush (*Olearia argophylla*), and the shrubs and trees with the deep green foliage and dark trunks and branches are blackwood (*Acacia melanoxylon*).

*T*he superb lyrebird (*Menura novaehollandiae*) is commonly found in the damper subalpine regions of the Australian Alps. This is a male of the species, distinguished by its wonderful harplike tail of sixteen feathers which it raises and spreads out over its head during its elaborate courtship ritual. The female's tail is plainer and less manoeuvrable. The mound of soil on which this bird is scratching acts as a stage for the courtship performance in which visual and sonic elements combine to attract one or more females.

344

*T*he mountain grasshopper (*Acripeza reticulata*), one of the long-horned species, is found in mountain and lowland regions in Tasmania, Victoria and New South Wales. This female has its front wings spread in a defence display revealing the brilliant colours of its rounded body. The female mountain grasshopper is unusual among grasshoppers in that it lacks hindwings. The male has a slender body and has both forewings and hindwings.

*T*housands of Bogong moths (*Agrotis infusa*) cluster between rocks at Mt Gingera in the Namadgi National Park. During the summer huge numbers of these dull brown moths shelter in rock crevices and caves, often swarming at night between locations. The flesh of these moths is very nutritious and was a favourite food of Aborigines who during the summer months would gather especially to feast on Bogong moths. The larvae of these moths infest crops and are considered a major pest.

*W*hite tendril-like blooms characterise the alpine grevillea (*Grevillea australis*), a shrub that is common both in mountain and some lowland areas of Tasmania, Victoria and New South Wales. The species grows in various forms in different locations, and can be either an erect shrub growing as tall as two metres or, as is most common in alpine regions, a prostrate plant that spreads over the ground or rocks. In Victoria and New South Wales the alpine grevillea grows predominantly in alpine locations.

A group of silver snow daisies (*Celmisia sp.*) growing near Charlotte's Pass in the Kosciusko National Park in New South Wales. These flowers grow abundantly in the Kosciusko area and are among the most attractive of its summer blooms. The silver grey leaves, whose covering of hair may help them withstand the winter snows, are clustered at the base of the stalk which supports the flower about fifteen centimetres above the ground. As the plant ages the creeping stems spread and branch.

*A*mong the blossoms that adorn the higher reaches of the Australian Alps in spring and summer are the papery white flowers of the alpine sunray (*Helipterum albicans* ssp. *alpinum*). This perennial herb is found in the alpine regions of both Victoria and New South Wales at altitudes above about 1800 metres. The ones shown here were photographed on Mt Kosciusko. The opening flowerheads nestle among the silver-grey felted leaves or stand a little above them, but their stalks lengthen as the flowers mature to seeds.

*T*he bright red summer berries of the subalpine beard-heath (*Leucopogon maccraei*) are more eye-catching than the white bell-shaped blooms with tufts of white hair in their centre that preceded them (*Leucopogon* is from the Greek for 'white beard'). These plants are common in Victoria's Baw Baw and Bogong national parks and, unlike some of the swamp heaths that are common in the alps, grow on well-drained soils.

Right

*R*estricted to the Kosciusko area where it thrives in the steep rocky areas close to where snow persists for most of the year, the anemone buttercup (*Ranunculus anemoneus*) is shown here in a typical habitat in the Kosciusko National Park. With petals measuring up to three centimetres long, the anemone buttercup is one of the largest and most striking of all buttercups and, as the photograph shows, contrasts sharply with the smaller yellow buttercups (*R. niphophilus*) that are also endemic to the Kosciusko region.

One of the most distinctive of Australian trees, the snow gum (*Eucalyptus pauciflora* ssp. *niphophila*) is one of the few eucalypts that can withstand the severe cold of subalpine winters. With its trunks often bent and twisted into bizarre shapes from exposure to high winds and its variegated and changing bark, these trees have a special mystique.

This scene, in the Ramshead Ranges, gives some idea of the conditions in which snow gums, growing in an extensive stand in the middle distance, are able to survive. These trees can grow in a wide range of sizes and forms, from mallee-like profusions of stems to substantial specimens that can reach a height of twenty metres.

The
Subantarctic Islands

The
Subantarctic Islands

A southern elephant seal pup on one of the narrow beaches of Macquarie Island.

Previous pages
*T*hick, swirling beds of Antarctic kelp (*Durvillaea antarctica*) on Macquarie Island.

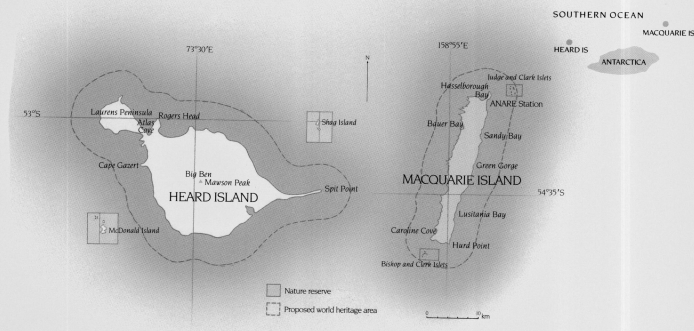

SOUTHERN OCEAN

MACQUARIE IS

HEARD IS

ANTARCTICA

73°30'E

N

158°55'E

Judge and Clark Islets

Hasselborough
Bay

ANARE Station

53°S

Laurens Peninsula
Atlas
Cove

Rogers Head

Shag Island

Bauer Bay

Sandy Bay

Cape Gazert

Green Gorge

Big Ben
Mawson Peak

MACQUARIE ISLAND

Spit Point

54°35'S

HEARD ISLAND

Lusitania Bay

McDonald Island

Caroline Cove

Hurd Point

Bishop and Clerk Islets

Nature reserve

Proposed world heritage area

0   10 km

Among the claims of the subantarctic islands to inclusion on the world heritage list are their importance as breeding grounds for penguins, seabirds and seals and the significance of their plantlife.

Until just over a century and a half ago these islands were the uncontested domain of birds and marine animals. The coming of sealers in the early nineteenth century not only almost destroyed several species of seals and penguins; it also paved the way for the introduction of rabbits, rats, cats and, as late as 1948, sheep and cattle, all of which posed a serious threat to the native flora and fauna.

Macquarie Island is notable as the habitat of the world's largest colony of royal penguins. It also has large numbers of king penguins and smaller colonies of gentoo and rockhopper penguins. Similarly conspicuous on the beaches, and contributing to an incomparable wildlife spectacle, are huge numbers of elephant seals and three species of fur seal. The seals and penguins are sustained by diverse marine life that inhabits the submarine shelf around the island. So too are the many seabirds that, as well as the albatrosses, include cormorants, shags and the great skua.

The more northerly Heard and McDonald Island groups have fauna similar to that of Macquarie Island. Although fur seals on Heard Island were almost exterminated in the sealing era, those on the inaccessible McDonald Island were virtually unaffected and are now helping to replenish the Heard Island colonies. Penguin species are dominated by the macaroni, which greatly outnumber the king, gentoo and rockhopper penguins.

Vegetation on Macquarie Island is sparse. There are no trees and the tallest vegetation is the tussock grass that provides protection for nesting seabirds. In the Heard–McDonald group the poorly developed soils support tussock in the lower areas. Above 200 metres mosses and lichens constitute the only vegetation.

Second in size only to the emperor penguin, the king penguin (*Aptenodytes patagonicus*), which grows to about ninety centimetres tall and is found throughout the Antarctic and subantarctic islands, exceeds its continental counterpart in the brilliance of its colouration. This close-up, taken on Heard Island, shows the vividly contrasted and well-defined colours that, with the long slender beak, give the king penguin its sleek appearance.

Below

A pair of macaroni penguins (*Eudyptes chrysolophus*), one of the two breeds of crested penguins that are widely distributed throughout the subantarctic islands but not found on the Antarctic continent. These black-faced macaronis breed on Heard and McDonald islands while Macquarie Island is host to huge numbers of the white-faced variety. Macaronis are distinguished by their bright orange plumes, the pungent odour they exude and their characteristically harsh braying noises.

Right

Large colonies of penguins are a feature of many of the beaches of Macquarie Island during the summer breeding season. It is only at Lusitania Bay, however, that the king penguins are to be found. In this vast colony the juveniles are instantly recognisable by their downy brown plumage. There are about 200 000 king penguins on Macquarie Island. Their numbers have been greatly depleted over many years by sealers, who have taken them for their plumage and blubber.

*T*hese small plants of helmet orchid (*Corybas macranthus*), barely poking through a bed of moss, are among the less common of the few hardy species of vegetation that manage to thrive in the relatively sheltered valleys of Macquarie Island.

*W*hen in summer blossom, green sage (*Pleurophyllum hookeri*) adds splashes of colour to relieve the predominantly green and stunted vegetation of Macquarie Island. Apart from the yellow-flowering Macquarie Island cabbage, it is the only plant on the island that produces eye-catching blooms.

*W*ithout its rusty red blossoms, green sage provides a lighter contrast to the brownish green tussock vegetation that covers part of the plateau of Macquarie Island. This plant grows extensively on the island from sea level to the highest peaks.

A male New Zealand fur seal (*Arctocephalus forsteri*) bares its teeth and barks aggressively to warn interlopers away from its territory. Males of this species, indulging in fierce territorial battles, often seriously wound each other with their savage biting. As its name suggests, the New Zealand fur seal, which is found on many subantarctic islands, is more widespread than most Antarctic species; it is very common around New Zealand.

An adult female Antarctic fur seal (*Arctocephalus gazella*) stands erect, firmly supported by her large flippers. Fur seals, sometimes called 'eared' seals because of their small earflaps, enjoy much greater mobility on land than do the earless or 'true' seals. The female Antarctic fur seal is shorter and lighter than her male counterpart which also has a thick mane of fur on its neck and shoulders.

Below

Despite their seeming ferocity, territorial fights like this one between two male southern elephant seals (*Mirounga leonina*) consist mainly of the combatants' hitting each other with heads and bodies and rarely result in serious injury.

Right

Moulting male southern elephant seals (*Mirounga leonina*), packed in a row like giant logs, on Macquarie Island. These huge marine mammals grow as much as seven metres long with a girth of up to four metres. Mature males of eight or nine years develop an inflatable trunk or proboscis through which the animal produces its characteristic loud roar. A male has a harem of up to thirty females. Each cow produces a single pup in October. Cows are significantly smaller than the bulls and are dark brown in colour.

*S*imilar in size to the Adelie penguin, but distinguishable by its white throat and cheeks, its more aggressive nature and harsh shrill cry and, most obviously, by the narrow strip of black across its throat, the chinstrap penguin (*Pygoscelis antarctica*) is distributed widely around the subantarctic islands where it breeds, as here, on rocky ground in a nest surrounded with pebbles. The adult in this photograph is disgorging food into the mouth of its chick.

A confrontation between two macaroni penguins (*Eudyptes chrysolophus*) on a beach on Macquarie Island, where there are about two million of these birds. The huge colony of macaronis at Hurd Point, one of almost fifty on the island, is the world's largest penguin colony. Macaroni penguins spend five months of every year — from May to September — at sea.

A vast colony of macaroni penguins and some southern elephant seals on a beach on Macquarie Island.

*T*he grey-headed albatross (*Diomedea chrysostoma*) breeds on the subantarctic islands and is found throughout the southern hemisphere. This one is incubating its single egg, on a nest of plants bound together with mud, at Caroline Cove on Macquarie Island. One of the smaller albatrosses, the grey-headed albatrosses nevertheless can grow to almost a metre in length and achieve a wingspan of more than two metres.

A black-browed albatross (*Diomedea melanophris*) and its chick on their nest of reinforced mud on a Macquarie Island hillside. These birds, one of the four species of albatross on Macquarie Island, breed on most of the subantarctic islands and are also common around the southern coasts of Australia. The chicks have dark beaks which change with maturity to the orange-yellow of the adult beak. The birds feed on a variety of fish and crustaceans as well as on carrion.

Previous pages

*A*lthough most of Heard Island is covered with ice, there are numerous ice-free parts of the island where a simple vegetation pattern has developed. This is restricted to a few species of vascular plants and a wide range of mosses, lichens and liverworts. Two of the most characteristic plants are the cushion plant (*Azorella selago*), which forms a rich green cushion over much of the rocky terrain, and the Kerguelen cabbage (*Pringlea antiscorbutica*).

A pair of wandering albatrosses (*Diomedea exulans*), one with its massive wings outstretched, perform a complex courtship ritual on Macquarie Island. Clumsy on the ground but magisterial in flight, this largest of albatrosses can have a wingspan of between three and four metres, the greatest of any bird. Courtship displays often lead to the formation of lifelong pair bondings.

*S*imilar to the macaroni, but with its yellow crest protruding at the sides instead of swept backwards and its eyes a bright red colour, the rockhopper penguin (*Eudyptes crestatus*) is both the most fiercely aggressive and the smallest of the crested penguins. It breeds on the more northerly subantarctic islands, including Macquarie and Heard.

*I*mmediately recognisable by their bright orange bills and by the patch of white that stretches between the eyes across their otherwise black heads, gentoo penguins (*Pygoscelis papua*) are more widespread throughout the subantarctic islands than the slightly smaller Adelie and chinstrap penguins to which they are related and near which they often breed. Unlike Adelies, however, gentoos do not breed on the Antarctic continent. This group was photographed on Macquarie Island.

Right

A colony of king shags (*Phalacrocorax albiventer purpurescens*), also known as blue-eyed cormorants because of the rings of blue skin around their eyes, on their nest on a rocky outcrop on Macquarie Island. This bird, the only cormorant species on Macquarie Island, makes its nest of seaweed and feathers bound together with guano.

The Macquarie Island cabbage (*Stilbocarpa polaris*) is one of only two plants with brightly coloured flowering heads that grow on the island. This plant, which is endemic to the subantarctic islands, is most prominent in the gullies. It is rich in vitamin C and was eaten by the sealers as a protection against scurvy.

The severity of the climate and paucity of the soil have resulted in a very restricted range of vegetation on the rugged Heard Island. In more elevated regions only mosses and lichens grow. This photograph shows lichen growing on a volcanic rock less than four centimetres in diameter.

Right

The luxuriant green of the cushion plant, *Colobanthus muscoides*, stands out against the predominant grey of the rocky shoreline near Caroline Cove on Macquarie Island. Further contrast is provided by mosses and lichens clinging to some of the rocks, by the colony of macaroni penguins and by the dull green vegetation covering the distant slope.

With its sleek hooded appearance and white eyerings the light-mantled sooty albatross (*Phoebetria palpebrata*) is perhaps the most strikingly handsome of all albatrosses. It is also the most southerly in its range and is the only albatross to be found regularly in the region of the pack ice. It breeds on subantarctic islands, usually on hillside ledges, and will often fly great distances to find food for its young. One of the smaller albatrosses, it grows to a length of about 700 millimetres, and has a wingspan of two metres.

Similar to an albatross, but with a distinctive curved back, a southern giant petrel (*Macronectes giganteus*) swoops across the water near Macquarie Island.

*L*ike its more southerly counterpart the Antarctic skua, the more stocky great skua (*Stercorarius skua lonnbergi*), which breeds on most of the subantarctic islands, is one of the most aggressively predatory of Antarctic birds. It commonly raids the nests and kills the chicks of the smaller species of penguins and poses a constant threat to seal pups and small birds. Its predations, however, are not always uncontested; here an angry king penguin fights back in defence of its egg.

*T*he kelp gull (*Larus dominicanus*) is the only genuine gull to breed in the Antarctic region and is found widely in the subantarctic islands as well as in more northerly climes. In the area around the Antarctic peninsula these large scavenging birds, which grow to almost 600 millimetres in length, sometimes persist throughout the whole year. This pair has built its nest around a cushion plant on a cliff on Macquarie Island.

Antarctica

Antarctica

A Weddell seal (*Leptonychotes weddellii*) emerges from a breathing hole in the ice.

Previous pages
Chicks gather for feeding in a rookery of Adelie penguins
(*Pygoscelis adeliae*) on Torgersen Island, off the Antarctic Peninsula.

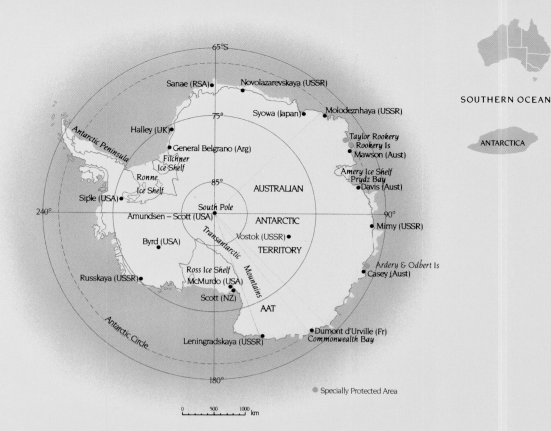

Apart from a number of minute invertebrates, the vast majority of which are invisible to the naked eye, the fauna of the Antarctic continent consists of penguins, seabirds and shorebirds, and marine animals. Only two species of penguins — the large and stately emperors and the small, swift-moving Adelies — breed on the shores of the Antarctic continent, and only the emperor breeds exclusively there. The Adelie breeds as well on several islands south of the Antarctic Convergence. Two other small penguins, the chinstrap and the gentoo, breed on islands close to the Antarctic peninsula, as well as further afield. While the Adelies are the most numerous and widespread of all the Antarctic and subantarctic penguin species, the emperors are the most truly continental, remaining on the shores right through the winter while their smaller counterparts depart to the relatively warmer environment of the pack ice.

In the warmer months six species of seabirds and two shorebirds breed on the Antarctic continent. Only two of these, the Antarctic petrel and the Antarctic skua, breed exclusively on the continent and its offshore islands. While the Antarctic petrel and the pure white snow petrel are among the few remaining on the continent the year round, the aggressive and predatory Antarctic skua travels north to warmer climes in the winter.

Several species of seals live and breed on the continent and its islands. Most familiar, because it frequents the ice closest to the shore, is the dark and blotchy Weddell seal. The most numerous is the crabeater which, despite its name, feeds exclusively on krill, the small red crustacean which is abundant in Antarctic waters. The most aggressive is the handsome leopard seal, a frequent and savage predator on Adelie penguins.

Mosses and lichens are the most widespread types of vegetation in Antarctica. These are most abundant on the western side of the peninsula where the milder conditions support the continent's only two vascular plants, a grass and a pearlwort.

Slightly larger than the more northerly king penguins, but similar in their colouration, emperors (*Aptenodytes forsteri*) are the only species of penguin to live and breed exclusively around the shores of the Antarctic continent. They can grow to more than a metre in height and are noted for their rigidly upright stance while they are moving, a bearing they abandon only if alarmed or threatened. The chicks in the bottom picture are moulting into their adult plumage.

Right

A solitary adult emperor penguin stands sentinel-like before the vast Auster rookery near Mawson on the east coast of the continent. The icecliffs that provide a majestic backdrop typify the settings of the twenty-five or so breeding colonies that exist around the coast, supporting about a quarter of a million breeding birds. The egg, laid in autumn, is incubated by the male who endures a sixty day fast while the female returns to the sea to feed. When the egg is hatched the female returns to feed and rear the chick.

Mosses cover rocks near the Australian station at Mawson. Thirty species of mosses are found on the continent. These and lichens constitute the two most common larger forms of plantlife — there are only two vascular plants, which grow on the Antarctic Peninsula — and are limited mainly to the ice-free patches around the edges of the continent and on the Antarctic Peninsula, although both kinds have been reported further south than 80°S.

Mosses are the predominant form of plantlife around the Antarctic coast. In some areas the melting of snow or glaciers during the summer creates meltwater pools, like this one near the Australian station at Casey, in which large beds of mosses and other plantlife can form. The resultant conditions in turn support myriad minute animals, most of them invisible to the naked eye.

*I*cicles hang like tiny stalactites from rocks in the crevices of which grows a yellow-orange species of lichen. Like mosses, the 125 species of lichens — composites of fungi and algae — that grow to the east of the peninsula are well adapted to the harshness of the environment because of their capacity to survive temperatures as low as −20°Celsius and their predilection for sheltered niches and even the pores and tiny cracks in rocks.

Adelies are fast movers on the snow and ice, being adept at both running and tobogganing. In the water they can reach speeds of fifteen kilometres an hour, propelling themselves forward with their flippers while steering with their tails and webbed feet. As they swim they often make porpoise-like leaps (*above*) during which they can breathe without impeding their progress. At right a group of Adelie penguins dive headlong from an ice platform at Cape Royds on Ross Island.

The Adelie penguin (*Pygoscelis adeliae*) is the most abundant and widespread of all Antarctic penguins. It is also one of the smallest, reaching a maximum length of about 70 centimetres. Distinguished by its flattened head and short, partly feathered beak, it typifies more than any other species the popular notion of the quaint penguin. The female lays one or two eggs in a nest of stones; incubation, and later feeding, are shared between the sexes. Here an adult cares for two chicks at the rookery at Cape Denison.

382

Basking on the pack ice in the summer sun, this Weddell seal (*Leptonychotes weddellii*) displays the light and dark blotches against a dark greyish coat that are characteristic of the species. Weddells, which grow to about three metres in length and can weigh as much as 400 kilograms, breed in more southerly regions than any other mammal. They spend most of the winter in the ice-covered sea, breathing through holes or cracks.

Below

The leopard seal (*Hydrurga leptonyx*) is named for its spotted coat, relatively elongated head and predatory habits. Leopard seals, which can grow to 3.5 metres long, are widely distributed around the Antarctic coast but breed mainly on the pack ice and are frequently seen on floes. The seal's teeth — the large incisors are evident in this photograph — are also well adapted to tearing the flesh of birds and other mammals.

*A*delie penguins on a floe near Cape Royds on Ross Island watch apprehensively as a leopard seal, the Adelie's chief predator, emerges from the water to lunge at them. The Adelie penguins employ both agility and cunning in their attempts to avoid the dangers posed by leopard seals. Groups of penguins will often wait until one or more of their number have 'tested the water' before diving; and Adelies being pursued can execute spectacular vertical leaps from the water to land firmly on their feet on the ice.

A crabeater seal (*Lobodon carcinophagus*), its normally greyish coat bleached almost to white by the summer sun, loafs with others of its breed on the ice near Cape Hallett. Crabeaters, which constitute more than 90 per cent of the Antarctic seal population and are the most numerous of the world's seal species, are preyed upon by the leopard seal and the killer whale. The crabeater feeds almost exclusively on krill.

385

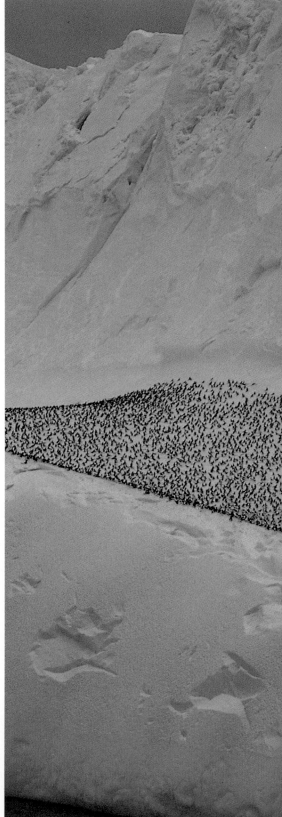

*T*he snow petrel (*Pagodroma nivea confusa*) is one of the few birds, apart from penguins, that inhabit the Antarctic continent all year round. Blending with its terrestrial environment and in startling contrast to the blue of the sky while it is in flight, the snow petrel rarely moves far from the floating pack ice. Beneath the pure whiteness of the snow petrel's feathers is a layer of black down that protects the bird from radiation from the sun. It nests in rocky ledges in cliff faces.

*M*ore limited in its distribution than the snow petrel, the Antarctic petrel (*Thalassoica antarctica*) breeds only on and around the Antarctic continent. Like its pure white relative, the less striking Antarctic petrel stays close to the pack ice and feeds on fish, invertebrates and occasionally the flesh of dead animals. It also has similar nesting habits, choosing covered or, as in this photograph, exposed ledges on cliff faces on which to hatch and rear its young.

A vast colony of grey and white
Antarctic petrels stands out against
the brilliant bluish white of a large ice
floe off the coast of Antarctica.
Exposed areas near the edges of the
pack ice, similar to the one shown
here, are the favoured gathering
places of these birds.

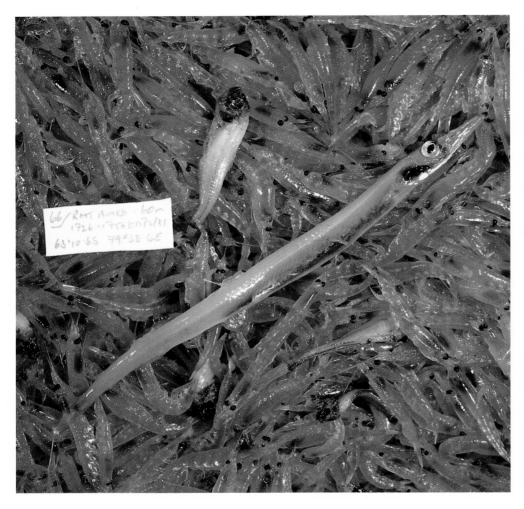

A catch of krill (*Euphausia superba*), the small red crustacean that plays a vital role in maintaining the ecosystem of marine Antarctica. Krill, which feed mainly on phytoplankton, tiny plants that float near the surface of the sea, are themselves preyed upon by large marine mammals, fish — several of which can be seen in the photograph — penguins and other seabirds. In recent years, and especially since the scaling down of the whaling industry, the protein- and vitamin-rich krill have been trawled, mainly to produce animal food.

A common sight during the Antarctic summer is of an Antarctic skua (*Catharacta maccormicki*) in full and majestic flight. This photograph clearly shows the power of this scavenger's large white-tipped wings and the strong webbed feet which it uses to good advantage in defending its territory. The Antarctic skua, the more southerly of the two species of skuas occurring in the Antarctic, breeds solely on the continent and migrates in winter to the warmth of the north Pacific Ocean.

Previous pages
The more benign climate on the western side of the Antarctic peninsula and the nearby islands allows for the growth of a more abundant and varied range of plantlife than occurs elsewhere on the Antarctic continent. The continent's only two vascular plants — a grass and a pearlwort — grow in this region, which also boasts more than twice the number of mosses and 20 per cent more species of lichen than are found to the east of the peninsula. This relatively large area of mosses and lichens was photographed on King George Island.

A pair of Antarctic skuas display typically aggressive behaviour against a potential intruder into their territory. Usually encountered in pairs, these skuas feed on fish and other marine life but also prey on smaller skuas and petrels and particularly on the eggs and small chicks of Adelie penguins. They establish their nests usually, but not exclusively, in coastal areas and often in the vicinity of colonies of Adelie penguins or petrels.

A minke whale (*Balaenoptera acutorostrata*) bursts through thin ice in order to breathe. Minkes, which grow to about eight metres long, are the smallest of the baleen, or toothless, whales that are regularly encountered in Antarctic waters. Baleen whales have horny plates in their mouths. These act like a sieve and retain small marine animals in the whale's mouth as water filters out.

A pair of killer whales (*Orcinus orca*), recognisable by their black and white snouts and prominent dorsal fins, ominously close to a colony of emperor penguin chicks. In the Antarctic killers prey on seals and penguins. They grow to a maximum length of about seven metres and are common in most of the world's oceans.

Right
*T*his photograph of the head and back of a southern right whale (*Eubalagna glacialis*) shows clearly the prodigious size of this baleen whale's mouth as well as the protuberances on its top and bottom jaws. Southern right whales are widely distributed throughout the southern hemisphere, but their numbers were severely depleted by whalers.

SPONSORS

Above

The morning mist swirls over Uluru.

tralia, and has attempted to confront geographical issues that involve this region. As a magazine we are committed to the preservation of Australia's wilderness. In fact, GEO began reporting on the ideology behind the world heritage list as early as 1979, with an article on the second World Wilderness Conference in Cairns, north Queensland. Therefore, it is with great pleasure that GEO supports our parent company's publication of this two volume collection — *Australia's Wilderness Heritage*.

JAMES HARDIE INDUSTRIES LIMITED

James Hardie Industries was founded one hundred years ago in 1888. It is now a very large trading and manufacturing group concentrating on the production and marketing of fibre cement and plaster building boards. Markets for these products are spread throughout Australia and New Zealand with a rapidly developing United States market centred in the Southern California region. It also has significant investments in paper merchanting and converting, fire protection, security and other building products. James Hardie Industries Limited is an enthusiastic supporter of the

inclusion of Australian sites in the world heritage list. The company is convinced that such listings will help to ensure their preservation and proper maintenance. The publication of these volumes, *Australia's Wilderness Heritage*, will also be significant in this respect and highlight the need to maintain constant vigilance if the natural beauty of our Australian wilderness is to be passed on to future generations.

QANTAS AIRWAYS LTD

Qantas Airways Ltd is proud to be contributing to the publication of this outstanding two volume collection of *Australia's Wilderness Heritage*. Qantas is an Australian company, now in its 68th year of operations. It has played a leading role in the development of this vast country and its communications with the rest of the world. Qantas regards the production of these books as a significant contribution to highlight the natural wonders of this continent in our Bicentennial year. These books are important to inform both Australians and the increasing number of tourists coming to this country about our unique wilderness and the varied flora and fauna that abound in it.

BIBLIOGRAPHY

Allen, L. and Harris, C. *Kakadu: Our Land, Our Heritage.* Weldons, Sydney, 1987

Antarctica: Great Stories from the Frozen Continent. Readers Digest Services, Sydney, 1985

Australian Wildflowers. Rigby, Adelaide, 1976

Baglin, D. et al. *A Treasury of Australian Wildflowers.* Ure Smith and Mulavon, Sydney, 1972

Barker, J. and Grigg, G. *A Field Guide to Australian Frogs.* Rigby, Adelaide, 1977

Barnes, R. D. *Invertebrate Zoology.* Holt-Saunders, Philadelphia, 4th ed. 1980

Béchervaise, J. *Antarctica: the Last Horizon.* Cassell, Sydney, 1979

Bennett, I. *The Great Barrier Reef.* Lansdowne, Sydney, 1971

Blombery, A. M. *The Living Centre of Australia.* Kangaroo Press, Sydney, 1985

Blombery, A. M. *What Wildflower is That?* Hamlyn, Sydney, 1972

Brennan, K. *Wildflowers of Kakadu.* The Author, Jabiru, NT, 1986

Brownlie, J. and Forrester, S. *Australian Wildflowers.* Currey O'Neil, Melbourne, 1982

Bullard, N. 'The White Lemuroid'. *Habitat* 15, 2, April 1987

Chippendale, T. M. *Wildflowers of Central Australia.* Jacaranda, Brisbane, 1968

Cochrane, G.R. et al. (eds). *Flowers and Plants of Victoria.* Reed, Sydney, rev. ed. 1980

Cochrane, G. R. et al. *Flowers and Plants of Victoria and Tasmania.* Reed, Sydney, rev. ed. 1980

Cogger, H. *Australian Reptiles in Colour.* Reed, Sydney, 1967

Coleman, N. *A Look at the Wildlife of the Great Barrier Reef.* Bay Books, Sydney, 1978

Costin, A. B. et al. *Kosciusko Alpine Flora.* CSIRO/Collins, Melbourne, 1979

Cribb, A. B. and Cribb, J. W. *Useful Wild Plants in Australia.* Collins, Sydney, 1981

Davey, K. *Australian Lizards.* Periwinkle, Melbourne, 1970

Edden, R. and Boles, W. *Birds of the Australian Rainforests.* Reed, Sydney, 1986

Erickson, R. et al. *Flowers and Plants of Western Australia.* Reed, Sydney, rev. ed. 1979

Gee, H. and Fenton, J. (eds). *The South West Book.* Australian Conservation Foundation, Melbourne, 1978

Goode, J. *Insects of Australia.* Angus & Robertson, Sydney, 1980

Gow, G. F. *Snakes of Australia.* Angus & Robertson, Sydney, rev. ed.1983

Hadlington, P. W. and Johnston, J. A. *An Introduction to Australian Insects.* NSWU, Sydney, 1982

Harris, T. Y. *Wildflowers of Australia.* Angus & Robertson, Sydney, 5th ed. 1962

Hawkeswood, T. *Beetles of Australia.* Angus & Robertson, Sydney, 1987

Hinton, B. and Hinton, B. *Wildflowers of Tropical Queensland: a Wilderness in Bloom.* The Authors, South Johnstone, Queensland, undated

Hodgson, M. and Paine, R. *A Field Guide to Australian Wildflowers.* Rigby, Adelaide, 1971

Holliday, I. and Watton, G. *A Field Guide to Australian Native Shrubs.* Rigby, Sydney, 1978

Hughes, R. (ed). *Australia's Underwater Wilderness.* Weldons, Sydney, 1985

Hutton, I. *Lord Howe Island.* Conservation Press, Canberra, 1986

Jones, D. L. and Clemesha, S. C. *Australian Ferns and Fern Allies.* Reed, Sydney, 1976

Kirkpatrick, J. B. and Backhouse, S. *An Illustrated Guide to Tasmanian Native Trees.* The Authors, Hobart, undated

Lane, B. and Davies, J. *Shorebirds in Australia.* Nelson, Melbourne, 1987

Lear, R. and Turner, T. *Mangroves of Australia.* University of Queensland, Brisbane, 1977

Macoboy, S. *What Flower is That?* Summit, Sydney, 1969

Meier, L. and Balderstone, S. *Kakadu: a Heritage for the Future.* Weldons, 1987

Messer, J. and Mosley, G. *What Future for Australia's Arid Lands?* Australian Conservation Foundation, Melbourne, 1983

Millet, M. *Australian Eucalypts.* Periwinkle, Melbourne, 1969

Moffat, A. (ed). *Handbook of Australian Animals.* Bay Books, Sydney, 1985

Morcombe, M. and Morcombe, I. *Discover Australia's National Parks and Naturelands.* Runaway, Sydney, 1983

Morley, B. D. and Toelken, H. R. (eds). *Flowering Plants in Australia.* Rigby, Adelaide, 1983

Mullins, B. and Baglin, D. *Western Australian Wildflowers in Colour.* Reed, Sydney, 1978

Murray, K. G. (ed). *The Alpine Flowers of the Kosciusko State Park.* Murrays, Sydney, 1962

Nicholson, N. and Nicholson, H. *Australian Rainforest Plants.* Terania Rainforest Nursery, Lismore, 1985

Ovington, D. *Australian Endangered Species: Mammals, Birds and Reptiles.* Cassell, Sydney, 1978

Ovington, D. *Kakadu: a World Heritage of Unsurpassed Beauty.* AGPS, Canberra, 1986

Peckover, W. S. and Filewood, L. W. C. *Birds of New Guinea and Tropical Australia.* Reed, Sydney, 1967

Penfold, A. R. and Willis, J. L. *The Eucalypts.* Leonard Hill, London, 1961

Readers Digest Complete Book of Australian Birds. Readers Digest Services, Sydney, 1976

Readers Digest Book of the Great Barrier Reef. Readers Digest Services, Sydney, 1984

Rotherham, E. R. et al. (eds). *Flowers and Plants of New South Wales and Southern Queensland.* Reed, Sydney, 1975

Serventy, V. *Australian Native Trees.* Reed, Sydney, 1984

Simmons, M. *Acacias of Australia.* Nelson, Melbourne, 1981

Simpson, K. *Birds in Bass Strait.* Reed, Sydney, 1972

Strahan, R. (ed). *The Australian Museum Complete Book of Australian Mammals.* Angus & Robertson, Sydney, 1983

Wade, P. (ed). *Every Australian Bird Illustrated.* Rigby, Adelaide, 1975

Williams, J. B. et al. *Trees and Shrubs in Rainforests of New South Wales and Southern Queensland.* Botany Department, University of New England, Armidale, 1984

Wilson, P. *Australia's Butterflies.* Kangaroo Press, Sydney, 1987

Worrell, E. and Sourry, L. *Trees of the Australian Bush.* Angus & Robertson, Sydney, 1967

ACKNOWLEDGMENTS

The contributors, consultant editors and publisher would like to thank the following people and organisations for their assistance in the preparation of this publication:

Ian Allison • Dr Peter Arnold • Australian Conservation Foundation • Australian Heritage Commission • Esther Beaton • Trevor Blake • Walter Boles • Gregg Borschmann • Keith Bradby • Laurie Capill • Gordon Claridge • Peter Clark • Conservation Commission of the Northern Territory • Conservation and Land Management, Western Australia • G. Copson • Phil Creaser • CSIRO and Lands Research, Alice Springs • Barry Day • Bruce Donald • Milo Dunphy • Peter Ewing • Rodney Falconer • Doug Ferrell • Sue Hand • Lisa Handley • Dr George Heinsohn • Roz Hinde • Colette Hoeben • Geoff Holloway • Dr Angus Hopkins • P. L. Keage • Daffi Keller • Dr Aila Keto • Ian Lock • Deanne Morris • National Parks Association of the Northern Territory • National Parks and Wildlife Service of New South Wales • Ken Newby • Simon Neville • Bob Pressey • Anne Robertson • Derek Roff • Ross Sadlier • Paul Scobie • John Sinclair • Ian Skinner • Jim Somerville • Dr Mark Stafford-Smith • Dr Alan Tingay • Dr Susan Tingay • Malcom Turner • Dr John Verron • Debra Wager • John Whitehouse.

PHOTOGRAPHIC CREDITS

Key t: top; b: bottom; c: centre; l: left; r: right

page 12 Densey Clyne/Australasian Nature Transparencies; **13** Grant Dixon/ Australasian Nature Transparencies; **14** J. Cancalosi/Auscape; **20** G. Wood/ Australasian Nature Transparencies; **26** Kathie Atkinson; **28** t,c, Leo Meier/Weldon Trannies; **32** t, G. E. Schmida/Australasian Nature Transparencies; **33** b, **34** c, Leo Meier/Weldon Trannies; **35** b, Kathie Atkinson; **44** t, **49** tr, Weldon Trannies; **52-3** Ron & Valerie Taylor/Australasian Nature Transparencies; **54** Kathie Atkinson/ Auscape; **56** t,b, Ron & Valerie Taylor/Australasian Nature Transparencies; **56** c, Australian Picture Library; **57** t, Pavel German/Australasian Nature Transparencies; **57** b, John Butler/Lochman Transparencies; **58** t, Ron & Valerie Taylor/Australasian Nature Transparencies; **58** b, Kathie Atkinson; **59** t, Fenton Walsh/Australian Nature Transparencies; **59** b, Australian Picture Library; **60** t, Fenton Walsh/ Australasian Nature Transparencies; **60** c, Kathie Atkinson; **60** b, P. Saunders/ Australasian Nature Transparencies; **61** t, Lloyd Grigg/Isobel Bennett; **61** b, Dean Lee/Weldon Trannies; **62** t, Kathie Atkinson; **62** b, Mark Heighes/Australasian Nature Transparencies; **62** cr, Cyril Webster/Australasian Nature Transparencies; **63** Dean Lee; **64** t, M. Prociv/Australasian Nature Transparencies; **64** cl Cyril Webster/Australasian Nature Transparencies; **64** cr, Kathie Atkinson; **64** b, **65** Dean Lee; **66** tl, Kathie Atkinson; **66** tr, Dean Lee/Weldon Trannies; **66** cl,cr,br, Ron & Valerie Taylor/Australasian Nature Transparencies; **66** bl, Fenton Walsh/ Australasian Nature Transparencies; **67** Ron & Valerie Taylor/Australasian Nature Transparencies; **68-9** Kathie Atkinson; **70** Ron & Valerie Taylor/Australasian Nature Transparencies; **71** t, Kathie Atkinson; **71** c, Fenton Walsh/Australasian Nature Transparencies; **71** b, Ron & Valerie Taylor/Australasian Nature Transparencies; **72** t, Dean Lee/Weldon Trannies; **72** cr,b, Ron & Valerie Taylor/Australasian Nature Transparencies; **73** Australian Picture Library/Volvox; **79** cr, Promotion Australia/ Australian Heritage Commission; **81** G. E. Schmida/Australasian Nature Transparencies; **90** t, I. R. McCann/Australasian Nature Transparencies; **90** b, **91** t, Kathie Atkinson; **92** t, Promotion Australia/Australian Heritage Commission; **92** b, Ken Griffiths/Australasian Nature Transparencies; **94** b, Graeme Chapman/Auscape; **96-7** Dennis Harding/Auscape; **98, 100** t, C. A. Henley/Auscape; **100** c, Kathie Atkinson; **100** b, Chris Bell/Australasian Nature Transparencies; **101** Jean-Paul Ferrero/Auscape; **102** t, Dave Watts/Wilderness Society; **102** b, Jean-Paul Ferrero/ Auscape; **103** t, C. A. Henley/Auscape; **103** b, Jean-Paul Ferrero/Auscape; **104** Ted Mead/Wilderness Society; **105** t, G. Cheers/Australasian Nature Transparencies; **105** c, Rob Blakers/Wilderness Society; **105** b, Ted Mead/Wilderness Society; **106** t, Hans & Judy Beste/Auscape; **106** bl, C. A. Henley/Auscape; **106** br, Kathie Atkinson; **107** Dave Watts/Wilderness Society; **108** t, Dennis Harding/Wilderness Society; **108** b, Kathie Atkinson; **109** Dennis Harding/Wilderness Society; **110** t, C. A. Henley/Auscape; **110** c, Dave Watts/Australasian Nature Transparencies; **110** b, Jean-Paul Ferrero/Auscape; **111** D. & V. Blagden/Australasian Nature Transparencies; **112-3** Jean-Paul Ferrero/Auscape; **114** t,b, Ted Mead/Wilderness Society; **115** t,b, Dave Watts/Wilderness Society; **116** t, Grant Dixon/Australasian Nature Transparencies; **116** b, Dennis Harding/Auscape; **117** Dennis Harding/Wilderness Society; **124** Kevin Deacon/Auscape; **124-5** Neville Coleman; **125** t,cl, John & Val Butler/Lochman Transparencies; **126** t, Adrian Davey/Australasian Nature Transparencies; **126** c,b, Ian Brown; **127** t, Graham Robertson/Auscape; **127** cr, Pam Gardner/Australasian Nature Transparencies; **128** t, M. Soper/Australasian Nature Transparencies; **128** cl, Ian Hutton; **129** t, R. W. G. Jenkins/Australasian Nature Transparencies; **130** t,c, Ian Hutton; **130** bl, M. Fagg; **130** br, Adrian Davey/ Australasian Nature Transparencies; **131** t,b, Ian Hutton; **131** cl, E. A. Pratt/ Australasian Nature Transparencies; **131** cr, Ian Brown; **132** t,c, Neville Coleman; **132** bl, Kathie Atkinson; **132** br, John & Val Butler/Lochman Transparencies; **133** t,c,cl, John & Val Butler/Lochman Transparencies; **133** b, Rob Littler/Isobel Bennett; **134** Graham Robertson/Auscape; **135** t, F. Gohier/Auscape; **135** cl John Hicks/Australasian Nature Transparencies; **136** b, Ian Brown; **138-142** t,c, Leo Meier/Weldon Trannies; **142** b, T. & P. Gardner/Australasian Nature Transparencies; **143-4** t, Leo Meier/Weldon Trannies; **144** b, Jutta Hosel/Australasian Nature Transparencies; **145** cr, Cyril Webster/Australasian Nature Transparencies; **145** tr,cl,br, M. Fagg; **145** tl, Ralph & Daphne Keller/Australasian Nature Transparencies; **145** bl, T. J. Hawkeswood/Australasian Nature Transparencies; **146** t, Ralph & Daphne Keller/Australasian Nature Transparencies; **146** b, Glen Threlfo/ Auscape; **147** t, Leo Meier/Weldon Trannies; **147** b, Ralph & Daphne Keller/ Australasian Nature Transparencies; **148** t, **149** t, Leo Meier/Weldon Trannies; **150** t, Kathie Atkinson; **150** cl, M. Fagg; **150** b, **151** Leo Meier/Weldon Trannies; **152** t, D. & V. Blagden/Australasian Nature Transparencies; **152** cr,b, **153-4** Leo Meier/ Weldon Trannies; **155** t, Jean-Paul Ferrero/Auscape; **155** b, Leo Meier/Weldon Trannies; **156** t, Ian Brown; **156** b, Ralph & Daphne Keller/Australasian Nature Transparencies; **157** Leo Meier/Weldon Trannies; **158** t, D. Knowles/Australasian Nature Transparencies; **158** c,b, **159-160** t, Leo Meier/Weldon Trannies; **160** c, Kathie Atkinson; **160** b, Dave Watts/Australasian Nature Transparencies; **161** Leo Meier/Weldon Trannies; **162-3** J. Weigel/Australasian Nature Transparencies; **168** t, Jean-Paul Ferrero/Auscape; **168** b, M. & I. Morcombe; **170-1** Denis & Theresa O'Byrne/Australasian Nature Transparencies; **176** t, Frank Park/Australasian Nature Transparencies; **176** b, Bruce G. Thompson/Australasian Nature Transparencies; **179-181** Jean-Paul Ferrero/Auscape; **186-7** Leo Meier/Weldon Trannies; **188** Hans & Judy Beste/Auscape; **190** tl, G. A. Wood/Australasian Nature Transparencies; **190** tr, C. & D. Frith; **190** bl,br, Paddy Ryan/Australasian Nature Transparencies; **191** J. Frazer/Australasian Nature Transparencies; **192** C. & D. Frith; **193** t, G. A. Wood/Australasian Nature Transparencies; **193** c, C. & D. Frith; **193** b, Hans & Judy Beste/Auscape; **194** t, Gunther Deichmann/Auscape; **194** bl Hans & Judy Beste/Auscape; **194** br, **195** t, Andrew Dennis/Australasian Nature Transparencies; **195** b, Ralph & Daphne Keller/Australasian Nature Transparencies; **196** tl,b, Leo Meier/Weldon Trannies; **196** tr, **198-9** Hans & Judy Beste/Auscape; **201** t, Weldon Trannies; **201** b, Ralph & Daphne Keller/Australasian Nature Transparencies; **202** t, Ian Brown; **202** b, Leo Meier/Weldon Trannies; **204** tl, Ralph & Daphne Keller/ Australasian Nature Transparencies; **204** tr, Klaus Uhlenhut/Australasian Nature Transparencies; **204** bl Leo Meier/Weldon Trannies; **204** br, C. & D. Frith; **205** tr, T. J. Hawkeswood/Australasian Nature Transparencies; **205** b, Andrew Dennis/ Australasian Nature Transparencies; **206** t, Pavel German/Australasian Nature Transparencies; **206** b, **207** t, Leo Meier/Weldon Trannies; **207** b, D. Whitford/ Australasian Nature Transparencies; **208** Ralph & Daphne Keller/Australasian Nature Transparencies; **209** Jean-Paul Ferrero/Auscape; **215** cl, Cyril Webster/ Australasian Nature Transparencies; **215** cr, Otto Rogge/Australasian Nature Transparencies; **215** b, Leo Meier/Weldon Trannies; **216** t, John Cook/Australasian Nature Transparencies; **216** b, G. E. Schmida/Australasian Nature Transparencies; **218** Leo Meier/Weldon Trannies; **219** b, Gunther Diechmann/Weldon Trannies; **220** John Cook/Australasian Nature Transparencies; **221** Leo Meier/Weldon Trannies; **224** C. & D. Frith; **225** t, I. R. McCann/Australasian Nature Transparencies; **225** cr, C. & D. Frith; **225** b, J. Gray/NPIAW; **226** b, G. A. & M. M. Hoye/ NPIAW; **228-9** Jean-Paul Ferrero/Auscape; **234** cl, D. & M. Trounson/Australasian Nature Transparencies; **234** br,Klaus Uhlenhut/Australasian Nature Transparencies; **235-6** t, C. & D. Frith; **236** c, Kathie Atkinson; **236** b, C. A. Henley/Auscape; **242** t, Leo Meier/Weldon Trannies; **243** t, Ken Griffiths/Australasian Nature Transparencies; **246** Hans & Judy Beste/Auscape; **247** t, D. & M. Trounson/Australasian Nature Transparencies; **247** b, Cyril Webster/Australasian Nature Transparencies; **250** Grant Young; **251** cl, Leo Meier/Weldon Trannies; **258** t, Jean-Paul Ferrero/ Auscape; **258** b, G. E. Schmida/Australasian Nature Transparencies; **259** t, Jiri Lochman; **260** br, M. & I. Morcombe; **261** tl, A. Krumins/Australasian Nature Transparencies; **261** tr,c, Leo Meier/Weldon Trannies; **261** bl, Frédy Mercay/ Australasian Nature Transparencies; **262** br, Leo Meier/Weldon Trannies; **263** b, M. P. Kahl/Auscape; **264** t, J. Purnell/NPIAW; **264** b, Leo Meier/Weldon Trannies; **266** t, Esther Beaton/Auscape; **266** b, Jiri Lochman; **267** t, M. & I. Morcombe; **267** b, Jiri Lochman; **268** b, **269** t, Graeme Chapman/Auscape; **269** cl, M. & I. Morcombe; **269** cr,b, D. & M. Trounson/Australasian Nature Transparencies; **270** Jiri Lochman; **271** t, G. D. Beste/Australasian Nature Transparencies; **271** c,b, Hans & Judy Beste/Auscape; **272** tr,br, Leo Meier/Weldon Trannies; **276** E. Parer-Cook/ Australasian Nature Transparencies; **278** t, C. A. Henley/Auscape; **278** b, Reg Morrison/Auscape; **279** tl, Dean Lee/Weldon Trannies; **279** cr, C. & S. Pollit/ Australasian Nature Transparencies; **279** bl, Weldon Trannies; **279** br, David B. Carter/Australasian Nature Transparencies; **281** t, Graeme Chapman/Auscape; **281** b, Jean-Paul Ferrero/Auscape; **282** t,c, Jiri Lochman; **282** b, A. G. Wells/NPIAW; **283** t, M. & I. Morcombe; **283** b, G. Harold/NPIAW; **284** c, D. Parer/Australasian Nature Transparencies; **284** b, Ben Cropp Productions/Auscape; **285** Roger Garwood/Photo Index; **286** t, Jean-Paul Ferrero/Auscape; **286** c, Jiri Lochman; **286** b, P. Röseler/Australasian Nature Transparencies; **288** t, Andrew Fraser/Auscape; **288** c, John Butler/Lochman Transparencies; **288** b, Robert Lawson/Photo Index; **289** t, Kevin Deacon/Auscape; **289** b, Michael Jensen/Auscape; **290** t, A. G. Wells/ NPIAW; **290** b, Mark Hanlon/Photo Index; **291** b, Kathie Atkinson; **294** Kathie Atkinson; **296** t, Otto Rogge/Australasian Nature Transparencies; **296** b, S. Wilson/ Australasian Nature Transparencies; **297** tr, Ken Griffiths/Australasian Nature Transparencies; **297** b, Kathie Atkinson; **298** Frank Park/Australasian Nature Transparencies; **298-9**, **299** tr, Leo Meier/Weldon Trannies; **299** c, T. & P. Gardner/ Australasian Nature Transparencies; **300** t,cl, **301-302** tl, Leo Meier/Weldon Trannies; **302** b, D. Whitford/Australasian Nature Transparencies; **303** Leo Meier/ Weldon Trannies; **304** tl, Graham Robertson/Auscape; **304** tr, I. R. McCann/ Australasian Nature Transparencies; **304-5** Marie Lochman; **306** tl, Graham Chapman/Auscape; **306** cr, D. & M. Trounson/Australasian Nature Transparencies; **306** b, B. G. Thomson/Australasian Nature Transparencies; **307** t, D. Whitford/ Australasian Nature Transparencies; **307** b, Kathie Atkinson; **308** D. V. Matthews/ Australasian Nature Transparencies; **309** Leo Meier/Weldon Trannies; **310-11** Jean-Paul Ferrero/Auscape; **312** J. Cancalosi/Auscape; **314** b, Simon Neville/Ecotones; **315** Jean-Paul Ferrero/Auscape; **316** t, Reg Morrison/Weldon Trannies; **316** b, M. & I. Morcombe; **317** l to r, t to b, Leo Meier, Leo Meier, Reg Morrison/Weldon Trannies, Hans & Judy Beste/Auscape, Jiri Lochman, S. Wilson/Australasian Nature Transparencies, Jiri Lochman, Hans & Judy Beste/Auscape, Jiri Lochman/ Auscape, Jiri Lochman, M. Fagg, Jiri Lochman; **318** l to r, t to b, Jean-Paul Ferrero/ Auscape, Jean-Paul Ferrero/Auscape, M. Fagg, Jean-Paul Ferrero/Auscape, M. Fagg, Jiri Lochman/Auscape, Leo Meier, Marie Lochman, Leo Meier; **319** S. Wilson/Australasian Nature Transparencies; **321** b, J. Cancalosi/Auscape; **322** t, Jiri Lochman; **322** c,bl, Leo Meier/Weldon Trannies; **322** br, Jiri Lochman; **324** t, M. & I. Morcombe; **324** c, Jiri Lochman; **324** b, **325** M. & I. Morcombe; **326** t, D. & M. Trounson/Australasian Nature Transparencies; **326** c, M. & I. Morcombe; **326** bl, Hans & Judy Beste/Auscape; **326** br, Jiri Lochman; **327** tl, Graham Robertson/ Auscape; **327** tr, Australian Picture Library; **327** b, Jean-Paul Ferrero/Auscape; **329** b, Jean-Paul Ferrero/Auscape; **330** cl, M.& I. Morcombe; **336** t, Jean-Paul Ferrero/ Auscape; **336** b, J. Cancalosi/Auscape; **337** Jean-Paul Ferrero/Auscape; **338-9** Harry Nankin; **339** t, Jean-Paul Ferrero/Auscape; **339** b, J. Burt/Australasian Nature Transparencies; **340** Jean-Paul Ferrero/Auscape; **341** Jean-Paul Ferrero/Auscape; **342** t, S. Wilson/Australasian Nature Transparencies; **342** c, G. E. Schmida/Australasian Nature Transparencies; **342** b, G. E. Schmida; **343** Jean-Paul Ferrero/Auscape; **344** Hans & Judy Beste/Auscape; **346-7** Kerrie Ruth/Auscape; **347** T. J. Hawkeswood/ Australasian Nature Transparencies; **348** tl, I. R. McCann/Australasian Nature Transparencies; **348** tc, Esther Beaton/Auscape; **348** tr, Denise Greig; **348** b, G. Cheers/Australasian Nature Transparencies; **349** Jean-Paul Ferrero/Auscape; **352-3** R. Williams; **354** Michael Mallis/Australasian Nature Transparencies; **356** t, Jonathan Chester/Wildlight; **356** b, Francois Gohier/Auscape; **357** Graham Robertson/Auscape; **358** t, Nigel Brothers; **358** b, Graham Robertson/Auscape; **358-9** Chris Bell/Australasian Nature Transparencies; **360** t, Otto Rogge/ Australasian Nature Transparencies; **360** c, D. Pemberton & R. Gales; **360** b, **361** Graham Robertson/Auscape; **362** t, Francois Gohier/Auscape; **362** b, **362-3** Michael Mallis/Australasian Nature Transparencies; **364-5** Jonathan Chester/Wildlight; **366-7** Graham Robertson/Auscape; **368** t, Michael Mallis/Australasian Nature Transparencies; **368** b, **369** Graham Robertson/Auscape; **370** t, Michael Mallis/ Australasian Nature Transparencies; **370** b, Jonathan Chester/Wildlight; **371** Chris Bell/Australasian Nature Transparencies; **372** t, M. F. Soper/Australasian Nature Transparencies; **372** b, Jean-Paul Ferrero/Auscape; **373** t, Michael Mallis/ Australasian Nature Transparencies; **373** b, Graham Robertson/Auscape; **374-5** Jean-Paul Ferrero/Auscape; **376, 378** t,c, Jonathan Chester/Wildlight; **378** b, Jonathan Chester/Australasian Nature Transparencies; **379-80** t, Jonathan Chester/ Wildlight; **380** b, Gordon Claridge/Australasian Nature Transparencies; **381** Jonathan Chester/Australasian Nature Transparencies; **382** t, Jean-Paul Ferrero/ Auscape; **382** b, Jonathan Chester/Wildlight; **383** Jean-Paul Ferrero/Auscape; **384** t, Mark Heighes/Australasian Nature Transparencies; **384** b, R. Williams; **385** Colin Monteath/Auscape; **386** t, Jean-Paul Ferrero/Auscape; **386** b, H. Marchant; **386-7** Jonathan Chester/Wildlight; **388-9** Jean-Paul Ferrero/Auscape; **390** t, R. Williams; **390** b, **391** Jonathan Chester/Wildlight; **392** t, G. L. Kooyman; **392** b, Don Croll; **393** Ben Osborne/Oxford Scientific Films

INDEX

A

Aborigines
  berrigan used by 87
  burning patterns 22
  Tasmania 99
Abrus precatorius 240
Acacia 39, 174, 273, 280, 290–1, 310–11, 313
  cyperophylla 302
  ligulata 292–3
  melanoxylon 344–5
  tetragonophylla 304
acacia 304–5
Acanthophis pyrrhus 168
Acanthorhynchus superciliosus 326
Aciphylla glacialis 339
Acmena smithii 145
Acrididae 172
Acripeza reticulata 347
Acrochordus arafurae 44
Adansonia gregorii 256–7, 261
Admiralty Island group 132
Aegintha temporalis 152
Aeprymnus rufescens 142
Agonis 313, 321
Agrotis infusa 346–7
Ailuroedus crassirostris 152
Aipysurus laevis 289
Albany 313
albatross 355
  black-browed 366
  grey-headed 366
  sooty 372
  wandering 367
Alectura lathami 147
algae 381
  blue-green 278
  green 132, 330
Alisteris scapularis 153
Allocasuarina decaisneana 174
alpine celery 339
alpine sunray 348
Alps 332–51
  evolution of flowering plants 18
amphibians 27
Amphibolurus barbatus 296
Amphiprion
  akindynos 133
  melanopus 54
  peridaraion 59
Amytornis
  goyderi 306
  textilis textilis 281
anaspides 106
Anaspides tasmaniae 106
anemone 54, 132
anemone fish 59
angel fish 72, 125
angiosperms, evolution of 16
Anhinga melanogaster 29
Anigozanthos 317
  manglesii 317
Anodopetalum biglandulosum 112–13
Anopterus glandulosus 105
Anous minutus 64
Anseranas semipalmata 30
Antarctic Covergence 377
Antarctic peninsula 374–5, 377, 388–9
Antarctica 374–93
Antechinus
  flavipes 324
  godmani 207
antechinus
  Atherton 207
  yellow-footed 324
Antheraea 159
  janetta 159
Anthias squampinnis 56
ants, green tree 239
Apogon aureus 56
Aprasia haroldi 290
Aprosmictus erythropterus 250
Aptenodytes
  forsteri 378
  patagonicus 356
Aquila audax 286
Archontophoenix
  alexandrae 202
  cunninghamiana 226
Arctocephalus
  forsteri 360
  gazella 360
  pusillus doriferus 106
Ardea
  picata 42
  sumatrana 41
Ardeotis australis 268, 306
Arenophryne rotunda 283
Argyrodendron 150
arid region
  eastern 292–309
  western 162–85
Arnhem Land 24–51, 267
ash
  alpine 332–3, 335
  mountain 116
Asplenium
  australasicum 150
  nidus 200
Atherosperma moschatum 109
Atherton–Daintree area, Queensland 21
Athrotaxis
  cupressoides 116
  laxifolia 116
  selaginoides 117

Auster rookery 379
Australian Alps, *see* Alps
Azorella selago 364–5

B

Balaenoptera acutorostrata 392
Balls Pyramid 129
bandicoot
  barred 277, 283
  golden 255
  northern brown 267
Banksia
  aemula 214
  coccinea 317
  sphaerocarpa 316
banksia 14
  fox 316
  scarlet 317
  wallum 214
banyan 38, 122–3
barnacle, goose 69
Barnardius zonarius 326
barracuda 288
Barringtonia acutangula 251
Barrow Island 255, 290
bat 27, 77
  ghost 271
  greater long-eared 81
  Queensland blossom 213
  see also fruit bat; mastiff-bat
batfish 72
Bauhinia 231
Baw Baw National Park 348
bauera 99
Bauera 99
bee-eater, rainbow 224
beech 96–7
  Antarctic 21, 141
  myrtle 99, 108
  red 241
belah 77
bell
  blushing mountain 318
  Cranbrook 318
  mountain 318
Bernier Island 277, 281, 282, 283
berrigan 86, 87
berrywood 131
bettong
  rufous 142
  Tasmanian 110
Bettongia gaimardi 110
bilby 295
  greater 308
billy button 335, 339
birds
  Cape York 231
  eastern arid region 295
  Fraser Island 218, 222
  Great Sandy region 213
  Kimberley 255
  wet tropics 189
birdwing, Cairns 190, 191
black bean tree 141, 144, 145, 157
blackbutt 213
blackfish, river 342
blackwood 344–5
Blechnum 136
Blepharocarya
  involucrigera 240
bloodwood 165, 185
blue lace flower 79
bluebell 79
bluebush 78–9, 79, 87
bluefish 125
boab tree 255, 256–7, 261
Boat Harbour 137
Bogong National Park 348
Boiga irregularis 206, 258
bolwarra, smooth 205
Bombax ceiba 240
booby
  brown 65
  masked 121, 134
booyong 150
Bossiaea foliosa 338–9
bottle tree 232
bottlewashers 180–1
bowerbird
  golden 193
  satin 152
Brachychiton
  australis 232
  discolor 145
brolga 50
brumby 213
brush box 141, 144, 151, 213, 221
Bubalus bubalis 48
budgerigar 170–1
Bufo marinus 245
Bungle Bungles 252–3
burr-daisy 166
  yellow 166–7
Burramys parvus 340
bush-pea, alpine 18
Busselton 313, 329
bustard 255, 268, 306
buttercup 335
  anemone 349
  yellow 349
butterfly 159
  brown 114
  mountain blue 190
  red lacewing 190
  wet tropics 189

butterfly fish 55
  black-backed 133
buttongrass 99

C

cabbage
  Kerguelen 364–5
  Macquarie Island 358, 370
Cacatua
  leadbeateri 76
  sanguinea 298–9, 299
Cacophis squamulosus 155
Caedicia 46
Caladenia
  discoidea 317
  latifolia 318
Calamus 200
Callitris glaucophylla 80, 88
Callocephalon fimbriatum 337
Calotis latiuscula 166, 176–7
Calotropis procera 261
Calyptorhynchus lathami 225
Calytrix 317
  exstipulata 261
camel 309
Camelus dromedarius 309
canary wood 249
candlebark 335
cane-grass 295
  sandhill 292–3
cane toad 245
Canis familiaris dingo 48, 309
Cape Denison rookery 382
Cape Hallett 385
Cape Royds 383, 385
Cape York Peninsula 10–11, 42, 228–51
Capra hircus 93
Caranx 125
Carbine Tablelands 195
cardinal fish 56
Carex 114
Caroline Cove, Macquarie Island 366, 371
Carpobrotus 330
  glaucescens 215
Casey 380
Cassina tenuifolia 118–19
cassowary, southern 193
Castanospermum australe 145
Casuarius casuarius 193
catbird, green 141, 152
caterpillar 91
  looper 238
Catharacta maccormicki 390
cats 129, 165, 355
Celmisia 348
Ceratopetalum apetalum 150
Cercartetus
  concinnus 14, 321
  nanus 110
Cethosia
  cydippe 190
  cydippe chrysippe 190
Ceyx pusillus 42
Chaetodon melanotus 133
Chaetodontoplus conspicillatus 125
Chalcophaps indica 128
Charadrius ruficapillus 222
Charlotte's Pass 348
chat, orange 298
Chelodina rugosa 44
Chelonia mydas 279
chenopod shrubs 77
Cherax 262
Chibnalwood Lakes 92
Chillagoe 231, 232
Chlamydosaurus kingii 34
Chlorodesmis 59
Chondropython viridis 206, 228–9
Chromodoris elizabethina 132
cicada 47
Cinclosoma castanotum 94
Cirrhipathes anguinus 72
clam 55, 60
  boring 60
Clematis 315
Clianthus formosus 166
climate, changes in 21
clover weed, purple
  purple 36
clown fish 59, 133
  black 146
coachwood 141, 150, 161
cockatoo
  gang-gang 335, 337
  glossy black 213, 225
  palm 231, 235
  pink 76
cocky apple 241
cod
  butterfly 57
  potato 55, 56
Colobanthus muscoides 371
conifers 18
  evolution 16
  native 96–7, 335
convolvulus, goat's-foot 215
coolibah 165, 295
Cooloola 213, 214, 226
Cooper's Creek 300
coppercups, summer 318
coral 55, 70, 132
  black 72
  brain 55, 66
  bubble 71

daisy 56
  encrusting 67
  foliose species 67
  gorgonian 55, 66, 72, 124
  hard 56, 66
  mushroom 66
  purple 67
  soft 71
  solitary 71
  xenia 125
coral berry 205
coral cays 55, 63, 64
coral reef 52–3
  Lord Howe Island 121, 124, 125
coral vine 310–11
Cordyline cannifolia 204
corella, little 298–9, 299
cormorant 355
  blue-eyed 369
  pied 223
Corybas macranthus 358
Corypha elata 231, 248
Cotter River 342
cotton tree, silk 240
cowry 60
crab, ghost 219
crabs-eye 240
Cradle Mountain 102, 105
Cradle Mountain–Lake St Clair National Park 109, 112–13
Craspedia 339
Crateroscelis gutturalis 193
crayfish
  freshwater 262
  land 106
  Mt Lewis 154
Crinea georgiana 322
Crinum flaccidum 304
crocodile
  freshwater 262–3
  saltwater 24–5, 27, 33, 255, 262–3, 264
Crocodylus
  johnstoni 262–3
  porosus 24–5, 33, 264
crustaceans 55
cuckoo, chestnut-breasted 250
Cuculus castaneiventris 250
Cunoniaceae 16
Curcuma australasica 36
curlew, eastern 212
currawong, pied 336
cuscus
  grey 231
  spotted 231, 236
cushion, snow 105
cushion plant 104, 105, 364–5, 371, 373
cyanophytes 278
Cyathea 126, 136, 161, 203
  leichhardtiana 143
cycad 6, 165, 184, 210–11, 315
  evolution 16
Cyclorana
  australis 262
  platycephalus 294, 301
Cyerce nigricans 59
Cygnus atratus 327
Cyperaceae 215
Cypraea cribraria 60
cypress pine 88
  white 80

D

Dacelo leachii 50
Dacrydium franklinii 100
Dactylopsila trivirgata 194
Daintree River 194, 196, 209
daisy 165, 335
  mountain 130
  paper 316
  silver snow 348
daisy bush, musk 344–5
Darling Range 322
darter 29
Darwinia
  collina 318
  leiostyla 318
  meebolddii 318
Dasycercus cristicauda 178
Dasyuridae 282
Dasyuroides byrnei 306
Dasyurus
  geoffroii 324
  hallucatus 49, 267
  maculatus 103
  viverrinus 103
dead finish 304
death adder, desert 168
Dendrelaphis punctulatus 242
Dendrobium
  discolor 202
  kingianum 156
  moorei 130
  speciosum var. *hillii* 156
Dendrocnide moroides 204
Dendrocygna eytoni 43
Dendrolagus
  bennettianus 195
  lumholtzi 195
Denham 289
D'Entrecasteaux National Park, W.A., 19
desert 22
Diamantina River 300
Dicksonia antarctica 108, 344–5
Dietes robinsoniana 131
Dillenia alata 241

dingo 48, 213, 309
Diomedea
  chrysostoma 366
  exulans 367
  melanophris 366
Diplodactylus spinigerus 322
Dirk Hartog Island 290
Discorea 38
Disphyma crassifolium 281
dolphin 213, 277, 288
Donatia novaezelandiae 105
donkey 309
Dorids 132
Dorre Island 277, 281, 282, 283
Dorrigo National Park 143, 151, 161
dotterel, red-capped 213, 222
dove, superb fruit 246
Downey Creek 8–9, 196
Dracophyllum fitzgeraldii 136
dragon 165
  angle-headed 198–9
  bearded 296
  Boyd's forest 20, 198–9
  eastern water 197
  Gilbert's 32
  northern water 34
  southern angle-headed 140
  thorny devil 173
  white-lipped 34
dragonfly 238, 239
Dromaius novaehollandiae 85
Drynaria rigidula 202
duck
  Burdekin 43
  plumed whistling 43
Ducula spilorrhoa 250
dugong 213, 274–5, 276, 277, 284, 285
Dugong dugon 284
dunes, Simpson Desert 295
dunnart 282
  fat-tailed 77, 90
Durvillaea antarctica 352–3
Dysoxylum pachyphyllum 131

E

eagle
  little 259
  wedge-tailed 286
echidna, short-beaked 91
echinoderms 55
eel, freshwater 244
egret
  eastern reef 64
  great 31
Egretta
  alba 31
  sacra 64
Elaeocarpus grandis 240
Elanus scriptus 299
Elatostema reticulatum 138–9, 161
elkhorn 143
Elseya latisternum 244
Elythranthera emarginata 317
emu 21, 22, 85
  chicks 85
emu bush, spotted 166
Emydura australis 254
Enchylaena tomentosa 180
epacrids, alpine 18
Ephthianura aurifrons 298
Epinephelus tukula 56
epiphytes 143
Equus asinus 309
Eremophila maculata 166
Eriophora transmarinus 46
Erscotts Hole 125
Erythrura gouldiae 269
Euastacus 154
Eubalagna glacialis 393
eucalypt 6, 27, 169, 174, 231, 335
Eucalyptus 273
  calophylla 320
  camaldulensis 184
  diversicolor 314
  gomphocephala 329
  jacksonii 328
  marginata 320
  pauciflora ssp. *niphophila* 351
  regnans 116
  terminalis 185
Eucryphia 16
  lucida 100
  moorei 16
Eucryphiacene 100
Eudyptes
  chrysolophus 356, 362
  crestatus 368
Euphausia superba 390
Eupomatia laurina 205
Eupomatiaceae 205
evolution 21–2
  flowering plants 15–18

F

Fairfax Island 63, 65
fairy basslet 56
Falco berigora 179
falcon, brown 179
fan flower 63
fauna
  Cape York 231
  evolution of 21
  extinct 22
  Kimberley 255

Lord Howe Island 121
New South Wales rainforest 141
Shark Bay 277
subantarctic islands 355
western arid region 165
wet tropics 189
fauna, endangered 99, 213, 271, 308
fauna, introduced 18, 48, 93
cane toad 245
eastern arid region 309
Fraser Island 213
Kakadu National Park 27
Lord Howe Island 121, 127, 129
subantarctic islands 355
western arid region 165
Willandra Lakes 77, 92
fauna, marine 213
feather flower
claw 317
woolly 317
feathertails 180-1
fern
basket 202
bird's nest 150, 200, 228-9
fishbone 217
man 108
swamp 203
water 136
see also tree fern
ferns 127
epiphytic 217
Ficus 204
leucotricha 38
macrophylla ssp. columnaris 122-3
virens 38
watkinsiana 150, 157
fig 231
cluster 204
Moreton Bay 122-3
strangler 141, 150, 157
velvet-leaved 38
finch 295
double-barred 247
Gouldian 269
red-browed 152
star 269
Finke Gorge National Park 165
Finke River gorge 175
fitzgeraldii 313
flatworms 154
floodplains 27
flora
alpine 16, 18
Cape York 231
Kimberley 255
Lord Howe Island 121
Macquarie Island 355
New South Wales rainforest 141
Shark Bay 277
Stirling Ranges 321
subantarctic islands 355
western arid region 165
wet tropics 186-209
flora, introduced 18
coral berry 205
giant milkweed 261
Kakadu National Park 27
Lord Howe Island 16
flycatcher, brown-tailed 255, 269
flying fox
black 271
little red 49
forests
Antarctic beech 21
cloud 127
sclerophyll 21
temperate 21
fox 92, 165, 306
Franklin River 99
Fraser Island 210-11, 213, 220
fauna 218
flora 215, 216
Fregata ariel 62
frigatebird 55
lesser 62
frog 262
bell 148-9
burrowing 45
corroboree 335, 343
Fletcher's forest 149
rocket 226
sandhill 277, 283
water-holding 294, 295, 301
wood 243
frogmouth, marbled 247
frogs
Kakadu National Park 27
western arid region 165
wet tropics 189
fruit bat, bare-backed 231
fungi, bracket 38
Fungia 66

G
Gadopsis mamoratus 342
gannet 55
Gardenia 273
garfish 125
gecko 129, 165, 183
Bynoe's 297
knob-tailed 183
spiny knob-tailed 172, 258
velvet 255, 270
western spiny-tailed 322
Geometridae 238
gibber desert 303
gibber plains 295
gidgee 295
glider
greater 341

yellow-bellied 213
Glycichaera fallax 234
goanna 165
Gould's 34, 162-3, 301
lace monitor 227
perentie 182-3
sand 34
goat, feral 93
Gondwana 15-18
Gonocephalus
boydii 20, 198-9
spinipes 140
goose
green pygmy 40
magpie 30
Gordon River 99, 101
gorgonian coral, see coral, gorgonian
gorgonin 66
Gossypium sturtianum 180
Gould, John 269, 337
grass
porcupine 77
snow 335, 338-9
tussock 308
grass tree 96-7, 214, 321
grasshopper
long-horned 46
mountain 347
short-horned 46, 47, 172
grassland 27, 335
grasswren
Eyrean 295, 306
thick-billed 281
Great Barrier Reef 52-73
Great Barrier Reef Marine Park 64
Great Sandy region 210-27
Great Sandy Strait 213
Grevillea 313
australis 348
dryandri 36
eriostachya 167
grevillea 165, 261, 335
alpine 18, 348
Dryander's 36
flame 167
groundsel bush 79
Grus rubicundus 342
Gudeoconcha sophiae 127
guinea tree, golden 241
gull 55
kelp 373
Pacific 287
gum
mountain 332-3
red 255
river red 165, 184, 295, 300
scribbly 213
snow 18, 335, 338-9, 350-1, 351
swamp 116
Gympie 204

H
Haematopus ostralegus 218
Hakea 166, 313, 321
eyreana 166
victoria 318
hakea, royal 318
Halcyon chloris 264
Haliaeetus leucogaster 286
Haliastur
indus 223
sphenurus 234
Hamelin Pool 277, 278, 285
Hardenbergia comptoniana 315
hare-wallaby
banded 277, 282
rufous 277, 281
spectacled 236
Harts Range 165
Heard Island 355, 356, 364-5
heath 335
climbing 100
Hedyscepe canterburyana 126
Helicarion 158
Helipterum
albicans ssp. alpinum 348
roseum 316
Helmholtzia glaberrima 138-9
Hemiandra pungens 318
Hemibelideus lemuroides 195
heron
great-billed 41
nankeen night 40
pied 42
Heron Island 72
Heterodendrum oleifolium 88-9
Heteronotia binoei 297
Heteronympha cordace 114
hibiscus 165
mangrove 201
Hibiscus tiliaceus 201
Hickmania troglodytes 114
Hieraaetus morphnoides 259
Hill River 329
Himantopus himantopus 28
honey, leatherwood 100
honeyeater
green-backed 231, 234
horizontal scrub 112-13
hovea, alpine 338-9
Hovea purpurea var. montana 338-9
Howea forsteriana 122-3
Hurd Point, Macquarie Island 362
Hybanthus enneaspermus 36
Hydrurga leptonyx 384
Hylidae 196

I
ibis, glossy 31
Idiospermum australiense 205

Innisfail 232
insects 46
invertebrates, marine 68-9
Ipomoea pescaprae 215
Irediparra gallinacea 23
Iron Ranges 231
island apple 131
Isoodon macrourus 267

J
jabiru 51
jacana, comb-crested 23
jarrah 320
jarrah forest 310-11, 313
jasmine 38
Jasminum 38
jellyfish 218

K
Kakadu 24-51
Kalambaru 255
kangaroo 21, 22
eastern grey 334
red 22, 82, 165
short-faced 282
western grey 77, 82-3, 325
kangaroo paw 317
red and green 317
karri 314
karri forest 313, 314, 315
katydid 46
kelp, Antarctic 352-3
Kennedia coccinea 310-11
Kimberley 252-73
King George Island 388-9
kingfisher
collared 264
little 42
paradise 192
kite
Brahminy 213, 223
letter-winged 299
whistling 234
koala 7
kookaburra, blue-winged 50
Kosciusko area 342
Kosciusko National Park 339, 348, 349
kowari 295, 306
krill 377, 385, 390
kurrajong, sticky 261

L
lace bark 141, 144, 145
Lagarostrobos [Dacrydium] franklinii 100
lagoons 40
Lagorchestes
conspicillatus 236
hirsutus 281
Lagostrophus fasciatus 282
Lake Eyre 300
Lake Panban 79
Lakefield National Park 237
lambstails 180-1
Larus
dominicanus 373
pacificus 287
Laura Basin 248
laurel, native 105
leatherwood tree 100
Lebatanthus 100
lechenaultia, red 317
Lechenaultia formosa 317
Lechriodus fletcheri 149
Leichhardt tree 249
Leilopisma lichenigerum 129
Leptonychotes weddellii 376, 384
Leptoria phrygia 66
Leucopogon maccraei 348
Leucosarcia melanoleuca 153
Lialis burtonis 90
liane 226
Liasis olivaceus 35, 260
lichen 355, 364-5, 370, 377, 380, 381, 388-9
Licuala ramsayi 200, 202, 233
lillypilly 141, 145
lily 241
Darling 304
palm 204
red lotus 28
wedding 131
Limnodynastes ornatus 45
Linckia laevigata 60
Linospadix
minor 204
monostachya 145
Litoria
aurea 148-9
bicolor 45
burrowsi 107
caerulea 45, 243
chloris 148
coplandi 196
infrafrenata 196, 230
moorei 322
nasuta 226
splendida 259
xanthamera 196
liverwort 127, 364-5
Livistona 252-3, 272
eastonii 272
mariae 165, 175
lizard
blue-tongued 178
frilled 34
Gilbert's dragon 32
legless 90, 290
sand goanna 34
shinglebacked 77
white-lipped dragon 34

see also dragon
lizards
Kakadu National Park 27
Kimberley 255
Lord Howe Island 129
western arid region 165
Lobodon carcinophagus 385
lobster, painted spiny 61
Lockerbie Scrub, Cape York 10-11, 17, 240, 244
Loimia medusa 68
longicorn beetle 129
Lophognathus gilberti 32
Lophostemon confertus 144, 151
Lord Howe Island 118-37
evolution of rainforest flora 16
introduced flora 16
Lordhowea insularis 130
Lot's Wife 104
lotus bird 23
low herb 138-9
Ludlow State Forest 329
Lusitania Bay 357
lyrebird
Albert's 141, 145
superb 141, 145, 344

M
Maatsuyker Island 106
McDonald Island 355, 356
Macdonnell Ranges 6, 165, 175, 184
McIlraith Ranges 231
Macquaria australasica 342
Macquarie Harbour 99
Macquarie Island 352, 354, 355, 356, 361, 362-3
Macroderma gigas 271
Macronectes giganteus 372
Macropus
antilopinus 48, 237
fuliginosus 325
giganteus 334
parma 160
rufogriseus 102
rufus 82
Macropygia amboinensis 153
Macrotis lagotis 308
Macrotristria 47
Macrozamia
macdonnellii 165, 184
miquelii 210-11
riedlei 315
Maireana 78-9
pyramidata 79
mallee 77, 335
malleefowl 22
Malurus
coronatus 268
leucopterus leucopterus 290
splendens 326
mammals 22
Kakadu National Park 27
Willandra Lakes 77
mammals, marine 106
mangrove 189, 213, 231, 255, 264-5
freshwater 251
Manta birostris 288
manta ray 277, 288
marine worms 55, 58, 68
marri 313, 320
marsupial mole 22, 176
marsupial mouse 22, 282
Harney's 27
marsupials
Kakadu National Park 27
Tasmania 99
Willandra Lakes 77
mastiff-bat 155
little 155
Mawson 379, 380
Melaleuca
howeana 130
quinquenervia 214
Melomys
capensis 236
cervinipes 158
hadrourus 194
melomys
Cape York 236
fawn-footed 158, 236
Thornton Peak 189, 194
Melopsittacus undulatus 170-1
Menura
alberti 145
novaehollandiae 145, 344
Merops ornatus 224
Metrosideros nervulosa 130, 136
Michaelmas Cay 64
Microeca tormenti 269
milkweed, giant 261
Mimosa pigra 27
mimosa weed 30
minni-ritchi 302
Mirounga leonina 360, 361
molluscs 55
Moloch horridus 173
monitor 182-3
lace 27
Monkey Mia 288, 290-1
monotremes 91
Montipora tuberculosa 67
Morelia
amethystina 242
oenpelliensis 35
Mormopterus norfolkensis 155
moss 127, 355, 364-5, 370, 377, 380, 388-9
epiphytic 109

moth 159
Bogong 346-7
emperor 159
Mt Conner 176-7
Mt Gingera 346-7
Mt Gower 121, 126, 127, 131, 136
Mt Hotham 335, 339
Mt Kosciusko 18, 335, 340, 348
Mt Lidgbird 126, 136
Mt Weldon 104
mouse
fawn hopping 295, 302
Shark Bay 277, 282
spinifex hopping 176
see also marsupial mouse
mulga 295
mulgara 178
mulla-mulla 162-3, 176-7
tall 180-1
Murray-Darling river system 342
Myripristis 56
Myrmecobius fasciatus 312
myxomatosis 92

N
Namadgi National Park 346-7
nardoo 186-7
Nauclea orientalis 249
Nectarinia jugularis 234
Neds Beach 121
Nelumbo nucifera 28
Neochmia ruficauda 269
Neophema chrysogaster 115
Neophoca cinerea 330
Nephrolepis cordifolia 217
Nephrurus
asper 172, 258
wheeleri 183
Nettapus pulchellus 40
New England Tableland 342
Ninox strenua 225
Nitraria billardieri 84, 87
nitre-bush 84, 87
Noah Creek 205
noddy, black 64
Noddy Island 132
noonflower, coast 215
Normanbya normanbyi 202
Notechis ater 323
Nothofagus 18
cunninghamii 108
evolution 16
gunnii 96-7
Notomys
alexis 176
cervinus 302
Notoryctes typhlops 176
nudibranch 66, 132
numbat 312, 313
Numenius madagascariensis 212
Nycticorax caledonicus 40
Nyctophilus timoriensis 81
Nymphaea
gigantea 251, 261
violacea 260

O
oak, desert 165, 174
Ochrosia elliptica 131
Octopoda 219
octopus 219
Ocyphaps lophotes 94, 178
Ocypode ceratophthalma 219
Odonata 238
Oecophylla smaragdina 239
Oedura 183
kalumburu 270
Olearia
argophylla 344-5
axillaris 330
ballii 130
mooneyi 131
orb-weaver, garden 46
orchid 313
dancing 317
golden 202
helmet 358
king 156
lemon 318
moorei 130
pink enamel 317
pink rock 156
Queen of Sheba 319
Orcinus orca 392
Ornithoptera priamus euphorion 190
Orocyolagus cuniculus 92
osprey 213, 277, 286
owl
masked 270
powerful 225
Tasmanian masked 115
Oxylobium lanceolatum 315
Oxyuranus scutellatus 32
oyster shells with pearls 289
oystercatcher, pied 213, 218

P
Pachycephala pectoralis contempta 128
paddymelon (plant) 87
pademelon
red-necked 160
Tasmanian 110
Pagodroma nivea confusa 386
palm
Alexandra 202
cabbage-tree 175, 252-3, 272, 273
fan 189, 200, 202, 233
kentia 122-3
little walking-stick 204
mountain 126

piccabeen 213, 226
Queensland black 202
thatch 122–3
walking-stick 145
see also fan-palm; pine, screw
Palm Valley 175
Pandanus 203
  darwinensis 272
  forsteri 137
  heronensis 62
  spiralis 26
  tectorius 216, 220
pandanus 62
Pandion haliaetus 286
Pandorea 180
  doratoxylon 180
Panulirus versicolor 61
paperbark 189, 231, 255
  broad-leaved 214
Papilio ulysses 190
Parademansia microlepidota 296
Parastacoides tasmanicus 106
parrot 21, 295
  eclectus 231
  ground 213, 225
  king 153
  mulga 95, 170
  night 21, 295
  orange-bellied 99, 115
  red-cheeked 231
  red-winged 250
  twenty-eight 326
pea 165, 295, 313, 335
  Sturt's desert 165, 166
pearlwort 377, 388–9
Pelecanus conspicillatus 222, 287
pelican 4–5, 213, 222, 287
penguin
  Adelie 374–5, 377, 382, 383, 385
  chinstrap 362, 377
  emperor 377, 378, 379
  gentoo 355, 368, 377
  king 355, 356, 357, 373
  macaroni 355, 356, 362, 362–3, 371
  rockhopper 355, 368
  royal 355
  subantarctic islands 355
peppermint 321
  narrow-leaved 332–3
peppermint plant 313
Perameles 283
perch 125
  Macquarie 342
perentie 182–3
Peron Peninsula 290–1
Perth 313
Petasida ephippigera 47
Petauroides volans 341
Petaurus breviceps 111
Petermann Range 174, 180–1
petrel
  Antarctic 377, 386, 386–7
  snow 377, 386
  southern giant 372
Petrogale
  lateralis 168
  penicillata 340
Petroica
  goodenovii 88
  phoenicea 336
Pezoporus wallicus 225
Phaethon rubricauda 120, 135
Phalacrocorax
  albiventer purpurescens 369
  varius 223
Phalanger maculatus 236
Phascogale
  calura 324
  tapoatafa 49
phascogale
  brush-tailed 49
  red-tailed 324
Phoebetria palpebrata 372
Phyllodactylus guentheri 129
Physignathus lesuerii 197
pigeon
  brown 153
  crested 94, 178
  green-winged 128
  purple-crowned 246
  Torres Strait 250
  wonga 153
pigface, round-leaved 281
Pileanthus filifolius 318
Pimelea ferruginea 317
pine
  celery top 99
  hoop 141, 213, 231
  Huon 16, 99, 100, 101
  kauri 213
  King Billy 99, 117
  pencil 116
  plum 145
  screw 26, 55, 62, 137, 216, 220, 272
  see also plum-pine
pink fairy 318
pinkwood, evolution of 16
Pisonia grandis 64
pisonia tree 55, 64
pitta, noisy 147
Pitta versicolor 147
Pittosporum
  phylliraeoides 86
  undulatum 19
pittosporum, sweet 19
planarians 154
Planchonia careya 241
planigale, narrow-nosed 307
Planigale tenuirostris 307
Platalea regia 41
Platax orbicularis 72

Platycercus icterosis 326
Platycerium
  bifurcatum 143, 217
  superbum 157, 217
platypus 21
Plectrachne 280
Plegadis falcinellus 31
Plerogyra sinuosa 71
Pleurophyllum hookeri 358
plum-pine, mountain 18, 335
Poa 338–9
Podargus ocellatus 247
Podocarpus
  elatus 145
  lawrencei 18
Poephila bichenovii 247
Pomacanthus semicirculatus 072
Porphyrio porphyrio 41
possum
  brushtail 22
  common ringtail 142
  evolution of gliding 22
  green ring-tailed 208
  honey 316
  lemuroid ringtail 189, 195
  little pygmy 110
  mountain brushtail 142
  mountain pygmy 335, 340
  rufous ringtail 142
  scaly-tailed 255, 266
  striped 194
  western pygmy 14, 321
  see also ringtail
Pothos longipes 143
potoroo, long-nosed 160
Potorous tridactylus 160
prickly Moses 313
Pringlea antiscorbutica 364–5
Prionodura newtoniana 193
Prionotes cerinthoides 100
Proboseiger aterrimus 235
Proteaceae, evolution 15–16
proteas 15
Psephotus varius 95, 170
Pseudocheirus
  archeri 208
  herbertensis 188, 209
  herbertensis cinereus 194
  peregrinus 142
  pulcher 142
Pseudomys
  australis 307
  praeconis 282
Pseudophryne corroboree 343
Pteropus
  alecto 271
  scapulatus 49
Ptilinopus superbus 246
Ptilonorhynchus violaceus 152
Ptilotus 180–1
  exaltatus 180–1
  latifolius 176–6
Puffinus carneipes 128
pumpkin bush 131
pussytails 180–1
Pygoscelis
  adeliae 374–5, 382
  antarctica 362
  papua 368
python
  amethystine 242
  green 206, 228–9
  Oenpelli 35
  olive 35, 260

Q
quail-thrush, chestnut 94
quandong, blue 240
quokka 313, 329
quoll
  eastern 103
  northern 49, 267
  spotted-tailed 103
  western 324

R
rabbits 77, 92, 165, 355
Rainbow Beach 216
rainbow-fish 216
rainforest 21, 27
  Cape York 231
  cool temperate 141
  evolution 16
  Fraser Island 217
  Gondwana 16
  Kimberley 255
  Lord Howe Island 121, 126
  New South Wales 138–61
  subtropical 2–3, 141
  Tasmania 99
  warm temperate 141
  wet tropics 8–9, 186–209
ram's horn shell 69
Ramshead Ranges 350–1
Rana daemeli 243
Ranunculus
  anemoneus 349
  niphophilus 349
rat
  bush 158
  long-haired 299
  plains 295, 307
rat-kangaroo
  musky 21
rats 129, 355
Rattus fuscipes 158
reef, *see* coral reef
regelia, barrens 318

Regelia velutina 318
reptiles
  Kakadu National Park 27
  Shark Bay 277
  wet tropics 189
  Willandra Lakes 77
Rhadinocentrus ornatus 216
Rhododendron lochiae 201
Richea
  pandanifolia 96–7
  scoparia 105
Ricinocarpos pinifolius 215
ringnecks, Port Lincoln 326
ringtail
  green 21
  Herbert River 188, 194, 209
  rufous 142
Rivina humulis 205
Roach Island 134
robin
  flame 336
  red-capped 88
rock-rat, common 266
rose, mountain 130, 136
rosella, western 326
rosewood 77, 88–9
Rosewood Creek, Dorrigo National Park 161
Ross Island 383, 385
Rottnest Island 313, 329

S
sage, green 358, 358–9
salmon 125
saltbush 77, 78–9, 79, 92, 295
Salvinia molesta 27
Sarcophilus harrisii 98
Sarcophyton trocheliophorium 71
sassafras 99, 109, 141, 145
satinay 213, 221
savannah woodland 22, 189, 231
Scaevola taccada 63
scarab beetle 46
Schefflera actinophylla 203
Schelhammera multiflora 241
Sclerolaena 92
sclerophyll forest 16, 22, 189, 213
  Australian alps 18, 335
  scoparia, prickly-leaved 105
Scorpaena cookii 133
scorpion 297
scorpion fish 55, 133
  Cook's 133
Scorpiones 297
Scutelleridae 46
Scyphozoa 218
sea eagle
  white-bellied 277, 286
sea fans 66, 73
sea-lion, Australian 330
sea slug, sacoglossan 55
sea star 132
  blue 60
sea whips 66
seabirds 55, 64
  Antarctic 377
  Cape York 231
  Lord Howe Island 121
  Shark Bay 277
  subantarctic islands 355
seagrass 213, 274–5, 277, 284
seal 355
  Antarctic fur 360
  Australian fur 106
  crabeater 377, 385
  elephant 355
  fur 355
  leopard 377, 384, 385
  New Zealand fur 360
  southern elephant 354, 360, 361, 362–3
  Weddell 376, 377, 384
Seary's Creek 216
seasnake, olive 289
sedge 114, 215
  Tasmania 99
Senecio
  lautus 79
  magnificus 180
Serpulidae 58
Setonix brachyurus 329
shag 355
  king 369
shark 277
Shark Bay 274–91
she-oaks 189
shearwater 55
  flesh-footed 128
Shelburne Bay 241
shield bugs 46
shingleback 277, 291
shrimp 69
  freshwater 244
  mantis 69
  Tasmanian mountain 106
Simpson Desert 292–3, 295, 300, 302, 304–5, 306
skink 129, 165, 291
  alpine water 342
skua
  Antarctic 377, 390, 391
  great 355, 373
Sminthopsis
  crassicaudata 90
  dolichura 282
snail 158
  land 300
snake 27
  black tiger 323
  crowned 155
  fierce 296

file 44
taipan 32
  see also tree snake
snake-lizard
  Burton's 90
snakebush 318
Snowy River 335
Snowy River gorge 340
Sophora howinsula 130
Southwest National Park 106
sphagnum bog 335
Sphenomorphus kosciuskoi 342
Sphyraena 288
spider
  scorpion 297
  Tasmanian Cave 21, 114
spinebill, western 326
spinifex 77, 165, 176–7, 178, 255, 277, 295, 308
Spirobranchus giganteus 58
Spirula spirula 69
sponge 61
spoonbill, royal 41
squirrel fish 56
staghorn 217
starflower 317
Stegonotus cucullatus 207
Stenochlaena palustris 203
Stercorarius skua lonnbergi 373
Sterculia viscidula 261
Sterna
  bergii 64, 218
  fuscata 135
Stilbocarpa polaris 370
stilt, pied 28
stinging shrub 204
Stirling Ranges 321, 323
stork, black-necked 51
stromatolites, algal 277, 278
stromb, red-mouthed 132
Strombus luhuanus 132
Sturt's desert pea 180
Sturt's desert rose 180
Sturt's Stony Desert 295
Styx valley 116
subantarctic islands 352–73
sugar glider 111
Sula
  dacytlatra 134
  leucogaster 65
sunbird, yellow-bellied 234
swainsona, downy 304
Swainsona swainsonioides 304
swamphen 41
swamps 27
swan, black 327
sword-leaved plant 138–9
syncarids 99, 106
Syncarpia hillii 221

T
Tachyglossus aculeatus 91
Tadorna radjah 43
taipan snake 32
Tanysiptera sylvia 192
Tarsipes 316
Tasmania, western and central 96–117
Tasmanian devil 98
tea tree 99
  Lord Howe 130
Tecomanthe hillii 226
Terania Creek 151
tern 55
  crested 64, 218
  sooty 135
ternlet, grey 121
Tetragonia 330
Tettigoniidae 46
Thalassoica antarctica 386
Thelymitra
  antennifera 318
  variegata 319
Thornton Peak 194, 209
thorny devil 173
thylacine 22
Thylogale
  billardierii 110
  thetis 160
tidal mudflats 264–5
Tiliqua occipitalis 178
tingle, red 313, 328
Torgersen Island 374–5
Trachydosaurus rugosus 291
Trachymene coerulea 317
tree fern 108, 126, 136, 143, 161, 203, 344–5
tree frog
  Burrow's 107
  giant 230
  giant green 196
  green 45, 148, 196, 243, 259
  northern dwarf 45
  saxicoline 44
tree kangaroo 22
  Bennett's 195
  Lumholtz's 21, 195
tree snake
  brown 206, 258
  common 242
trevally 125
Trianthema megasperma 37
Tribulopis bicolor 261
Tricholimnas sylvestris 127
Trichosurus caninus 142
Tridacna 60
  crocea 60
Triodia 280
Trochodesma zeylanicum 176–7
tropicbird, red-tailed 120, 135
trumpet fish 55

tuart 313, 329
Tubastrea aurea 56
tubeworm, spiral 58
Tunnel Creek 262
turkey, brush 147
turkey bush 261
Tursiops truncatus 288
turtle 213, 254
  albino green 279
  freshwater 27
  green 277, 279
  loggerhead 277
  northern snake-necked 44
  saw-shelled 244
  turtle weed 59
tussock grass 255, 280, 308, 355
Tyto
  novaehollandiae 270
  novaehollandiae castanops 115

U
Uluru 167
umbrella tree, Queensland 203
Uraria cylindracea 36

V
Varanus
  giganteus 182–3
  gouldii 301
  panoptes 34
  varius 227
Verticordia
  grandiflora 317
  monadelpha 317
Vesselowskya 16
Victorian Alps 339, 340
violet 36
Vombatus ursinus 102
Vulpes vulpes 92

W
waddy wood 295
Wahlenbergia 79
wallaby 22, 77
  Bennett's 102
  black-footed rock 168
  brush-tailed rock 335, 340
  parma 160
  rock 165, 255
  toolache 22
wallaroo 77
  antilopine 27, 48, 237
  common 82–3, 165
wallum 214
Walpole-Nornalup National Park 328
Warren National Park 315
Washpool National Park 150
water buffalo 27, 48
  threatens magpie goose's habitat 30
waterbirds, Kakadu National Park 27
waterlily 40, 251, 255, 260, 261
wattle 39, 280, 295, 310–11
  dune 292–3
  sandhill 295
wedding bush 215
weeds, *see* flora, introduced
Weld River 108
Western Australia, southwest 310–31, 316
  evolution of flowering plants 16–18
  wet tropics 186–209
whale 277
  killer 392
  minke 392
  southern right 393
whistler, Lord Howe Island golden 128
Wild Rivers National Park 101
wildflowers
  Australian alps 335
  Shark Bay 277
  southwest Western Australia 313, 316
  Willandra Lakes 76–95
William Bay National Park 330
willow, native 315
Willowie Scrub 150
wisteria, native 315
wombat, common 102
woodhen, Lord Howe Island 121, 127
woodland 22, 27
Wooramel River 284
Wooramel seagrass bank 284
worm
  Christmas tree 58
  phyllodocid 68
  spiral tubeworm 58
  terebellid 68
wrasse, hump-headed 133
wren
  Australian fern 193
  desert 22
  purple-crowned 268
  splendid 315
  white-winged fairy 290
Wyulda squamicaudata 266
Wyuna Creek 216, 220

X
Xanthorrhoea 321
  fulva 214
Xenia elongata 125
Xenorhynchus asiaticus 51

Y
yabby 262
yam 38
yellowtop 180

Z
Zygochloa paradoxa 292–3
Zyzomys argurus 266
  see also grasswren